"If you ever paused to wonder whether or not God loved your city, your community, your street, your neighbors, Marty Troyer's answer is an unequivocal YES! The world God loves, the one Jesus died for, is right under your nose, and you won't see it the same way after reading this book."
—*Margot Starbuck, author,* Small Things with Great Love, *and coauthor,* Overplayed

"Troyer's *The Gospel Next Door* is a much needed work for the church, because it challenges us to be missional in our own backyards. This work gives believers a blueprint for how the gospel of justice can change not only our local communities but our walk with Yahshua through experiences of radical love."
—*Onleilove Alston, executive director, Faith in New York*

"*The Gospel Next Door* is an important read for everyone who takes Jesus' teachings seriously. Troyer is a trailblazer, and this book contains practical examples of how believers can make

an impact in their communities. Implement the principles in this book and start living out the kingdom here and now!"
—*Dave Runyon, coauthor of* The Art of Neighboring

"Marty Troyer has taken on the enormous task of helping us reframe the story we tell about what it means to do the work of the kingdom of God. He does that by thoughtfully examining the Scripture in the context of the mission field of Houston and by casting the story as both personal and community transformation. He does that with a pastor's heart and a prophet's urgency. And he does it as a wise, thoughtful participant in what God is doing in one of our nation's great cities. I highly commend *The Gospel Next Door* to you."
—*Jim Herrington, coauthor of* Leading Congregational Change *and founder of Faithwalking*

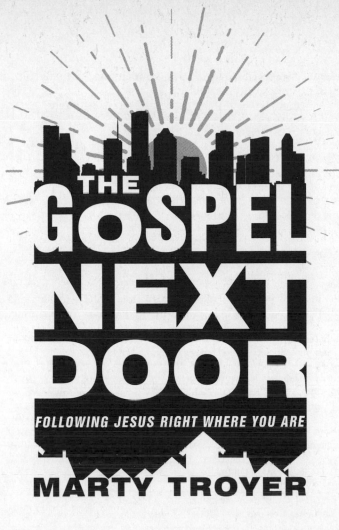

THE GOSPEL NEXT DOOR

FOLLOWING JESUS RIGHT WHERE YOU ARE

MARTY TROYER

Herald Press

Harrisonburg, Virginia
Kitchener, Ontario

Library of Congress Cataloging-in-Publication Data
Names: Troyer, Marty, 1976- author.
Title: The gospel next door : following Jesus right where you are / Marty
    Troyer.
Description: Harrisonburg : Herald Press, 2016.
Identifiers: LCCN 2016004643| ISBN 9781513800387 (pbk. : alk. paper) | ISBN
    9781513801032 (hardcover : alk. paper)
Subjects: LCSH: Evangelistic work. | Communities--Religious
    aspects--Christianity.
Classification: LCC BV3790 .T687 2016 | DDC 248.4--dc23 LC record avail-
able at http://lccn.loc.gov/2016004643

THE GOSPEL NEXT DOOR
© 2016 by Herald Press, Harrisonburg, Virginia 22802
    Released simultaneously in Canada by Herald Press,
    Kitchener, Ontario N2G 3R1. All rights reserved.
Library of Congress Control Number: 2016004643
International Standard Book Number: 978-1-5138-0038-7 (paperback)
International Standard Book Number: 978-1-5138-0103-2 (hardcover)
Printed in the United States of America
Cover and interior design by Merrill Miller

For orders or information, call 800-245-7894 or visit HeraldPress.com.

20 19 18 17 16   10 9 8 7 6 5 4 3 2 1

Dedicated to the six hundred thousand children in Houston, including my own: Malakai, Clara, and Ruby. May you always know you are loved. Never stop believing that a better world is possible.

Contents

Introduction: Following Jesus into a Neighborhood Near You . . . 9

PART I: THE GOSPEL AS LENS

1 How Jesus' Gospel Clarifies Pretty Much Everything . . 23

2 Borrowing the Eyes of God 37

3 Tell Them about the Dream! 53

PART II: THE GOSPEL GIFT OF JESUS

4 Look like Jesus. 63

5 Evangelizing Peace 79

6 Form a New Disciple-Making Culture. 97

PART III: THE GOSPEL GIFT OF PEACE

7 Shalom and the Common Good 113

8 Three Trillion Dollars of Potholes 129

9 Read the Bible with Black Lives Matter 149

PART IV: THE GOSPEL GIFT OF RESTORING JUSTICE

10 Houston, We Have a Problem. 165

11 Congratulations, You've Been Called! 181

12 Worship the God of Mission 193

Epilogue: Ship of Theseus. 203

The Author 207

Following Jesus into a Neighborhood Near You

EIGHT YEARS after Jesus accepted my invitation to come into my heart, I accepted his.

"Come, and follow me." It had been there all along, wild with dignity and waiting to transform me, his vision of me greater than I could ask or imagine for myself.

Looking back, it would have made more sense to invite him into my puberty, my past, or my plans. But heart is what I knew, and so heart is what he got. This worked out well, because it left a lot—and I mean a *lot*—up to me. I loved God deeply—on Sundays, during church, and when few people were watching. It was a deeply personal and controlled faith.

Had a friend asked me, "Are you able to leave your faith at church, or do you need to bring it home?" I would have happily responded, "Me? Nah, I'm able to leave it behind. I'm lucky."

Before I RSVP'd to Jesus' invitation, I did the best I could with what I had, pursuing things—American dream things—with gusto and the normal confusion of adolescence. I grew up in a fantastic home and was nurtured with all the resources of my faith community.

But I had not yet seen in myself what God could see: that I was deeply loved and needed in the world; that I was meant for a full life of abundance and flourishing; that I was being healed to become a healer; that God was alive and well inside me and the world; that the places of my deepest wounding would become my greatest strengths; and that in loving others I would never be the same.

My invitation to Jesus was the beginning of an amazing journey. But *his* invitation to me? Well, that was something else entirely.

Since then I've been hugged by atheists and condemned to hell by Christians, both for doing the same thing: sharing the gospel. There's never a dull moment when living life with God.

My atheist friend turned to me after I had prayed for the peace of our city in front of a large crowd. "I haven't prayed in decades," he said, "but tonight as you spoke, I felt something come alive." Those were words I could understand. I, too, had come alive when my invitation to Jesus was eclipsed by his invitation to me.

And then there's my Christian friend Brian, who threw his lunch in my face when I dared suggest God's will might not be wrapped in the Stars and Stripes.

Perhaps this shouldn't surprise us. After all, the gospel is about exodus and resurrection—life-altering, world-changing kinds of things. Healing the rupture in the fabric of human community and freeing us from what binds our souls isn't exactly work done in secret. So it's no wonder it stirs such deep passions within us and brings such transformation. That was the experience of the first-generation Christians, whose encounters with the gospel expanded their horizons. The gospel—God's aspirations for human community—turned fishermen into movement leaders, sinners into saints, enemies into examples, and ordinary people into partners with God.

This is still happening today. The gospel is transforming me from a shame-riddled young adult into an authentic man capable of receiving love and living it in my community. I see it in my family and in my relationship with my wife, Hannah. It's happening in the lives of the people I pastor, people who are experiencing freedom from selfishness, racism, and corporate greed.

The gospel is doing this before the watching world—a world our God values beyond belief, a world that God is healing.

FOLLOWING JESUS NEXT DOOR

This is a book for people hungry for a different spirituality and a better world. It's for those who are tired of being told discipleship merely means church membership or who are tired of needing to transform the world all alone. It's a book for missional communities that need clarity about what God is doing because they long to participate.

This is a book that speaks directly to my hunger to see myself and my community as God does.

This is a book for readers hungry to accept Jesus' invitation—"Come and follow"—and to go wherever he leads, even if it means following him next door.

Especially if it means following him next door!

Jesus led his followers all over his country and the next, into their cities, into the hornets' nest of religion, and into the homes of the most surprising people. Are these places you're willing to go, because God is here and Jesus is calling?

He marched on the capital without weapons of war and cleansed the temple while pious parents watched; he sauntered home to bring a dead man to life. These aren't exactly Christian music cruises in the Caribbean, retreats from the world for a little R & R. Jesus almost never went to worship without making people more uncomfortable than encouraged. Are these places you're willing to go, because God is here and Jesus is calling?

He walked past enemy lines, crossed borders, took field trips to forbidden cities, and climbed mountains to connect with God. Are these places you're willing to go, because these are the places that God loves and Jesus is calling?

If so, you're not alone. Thousands of churches, families, and missional communities are following Jesus right where they are and are being transformed along with their neighborhoods.

Ordinary Christians are putting their faith into practice—taking Jesus seriously, joining God in healing their neighborhoods, and refusing to remain silent about what they've witnessed.

This story does not come naturally to most of us. Most of us inherited a story about mission centered on foreign missions, which has to do with a sender (local congregation or mission agency) sending special people (missionaries) to a special place (over there!) to do special things (missions).

Ordinary Christians, in this model, are demoted to secular careers that produce tithes and to church membership that invites volunteerism.

But God invites us into a more nuanced narrative. The mission of God invites us to imagine a new *sender* (God) who sends *all people* to the *places they already live* to *restore all things*. No longer do we compartmentalize super-Christians who respond to God's call to go and second-class Christians who choose to stay.

Being a "normal Christian" actually means doing the very things Jesus would do if he were living our lives. True missional living invites us to imagine things differently: God, the gospel, the places we live, and our part in God's restoration project. If you sometimes feel as if your faith is not up to this new mission, I hope *The Gospel Next Door* will inspire you to imagine your city "on earth as in heaven," through faithful living and Christ-infused spirituality.

DOWNSIDE-UP DISCIPLESHIP

"Turning the world upside down" is how early witnesses described God's healing good news, the good news about a man who came preaching peace. These first-generation Christian women and men had been transformed from the inside out, not as keepers of a private God but as followers of a public way.

Abide in me, Jesus promises, and you will bear the kind of fruit that the world's great injustices won't stand a chance against, for this is the very work of God.

This invitation always comes with a location: a setting that roots our life of faith in a neighborhood or workplace or family. Jesus leads us to an address on a map where the gospel is already bringing life into the soil and streets and souls it touches. So too are we set free to partner with the mission of God in our world. "Peace be with you. As the Father has sent me, so I send you" (John 20:21).

Good news indeed, because that's exactly where we already are. Nothing universal, objective, or fair and balanced about that. The gospel is local, personal, and intimate, with a spotlight on the landscape in which you find yourself. And it turns our lives and world upside down. Or, in a world gone mad, perhaps it's turning all things right side up.

And how would we know? How would we know if our world needs to be turned upside down or right side up or inside out, or if we need a reversal of normal? How would I know if this is all there is to life or if a higher purpose is possible?

Because that address—that Google Maps pin dropped where your passions lie—makes all the difference in what God is doing and the mission of his followers. Our location profoundly shapes our mission. Churches filled with poor farmers pushed off family farms by agribusiness will put faith into action differently than Christians living intentionally in an apartment complex filled with recent Iraqi refugees. It's the same gospel applied uniquely to each setting.

If we cry "Peace, peace!" assuming that all is well when our communities are filled with the culture of death, we're as mistaken as the misled prophets of old (Jeremiah 6:14). Like them, the way we put our faith into action will likely be mistaken. Whatever form our social engagement takes, it is always shaped by our perception of the setting in which we find ourselves. At times in the Hebrew Scriptures, Egypt is seen as a place of great safety and peace, and at other times as a place of great violence and oppression. Being able to see the difference in our own context will clarify the shape of faithful witness.

In the first century, empire, oppression, and exclusive religiosity created a world desperate for inversion. The gospel filled this landscape with an alternative vision so different from the way things were that it shook the very foundations of life. But it did so in a way that was a gift of life with abundance (John 10:10). Not everyone embraced the gospel as good news, though it came straight from the heart of God. But for those who did—for followers of the Way—it changed everything.

Everywhere he went, Jesus understood exactly what people needed, and taught his disciples to see it too. Women need dignity, the poor need debts forgiven, the sick need healthcare, strangers need hospitality, leaders need to be provoked, and everyone—absolutely everyone—needs to believe the good news that God's kingdom of peace is now here.

Jesus saw his world through the eyes of gospel, and he is teaching us to see it too. It's a lesson that equips us with the proper lenses to clearly see God in the world.

This book is about that vision. It's about how to *see* differently through the lens of the gospel, which shapes us to *be* different and faithful and good. If we're passionate about making progress toward God's intended design, we'll need to understand exactly what we're getting into. The gospel can become a theology of sight for the neighborhoods and cities we inhabit.

This book, then, is not about *taking* the gospel next door, as if we bring goodness into empty space. This is a book about *seeing* the gospel next door, where God is already alive and already loving.

HERE'S WHAT YOU CAN EXPECT

By taking a tour of multiple landscapes, I hope we'll truly be able to see the gospel where we live, work, and play. We'll tour Houston, Texas, where I live, and cities and communities like yours. We'll walk around neighborhoods of decay and communities of justice, and we'll learn about the Scriptures' gift of human flourishing and culture's ways of stealing it. I'll let you in on stories of great pain in my life—or, interpreted differently, stories of great grace and growth.

And most importantly, we'll take a fresh tour of the everlasting adventure we call gospel. We'll shift our gaze from the effects of God's gospel to its cause, where we'll run full into the open arms of a welcoming God who acts in and for our world—the *whole* world. We'll see that the gospel is less about what happens to us and much more beautifully about who and how God is.

The chapters in part 1 ask the question, "What on earth is the gospel, anyway?" This part explores how the gospel can accurately illuminate the people and places in our lives so we can love well. As an eye doctor does when improving your vision, the gospel clarifies our world.[1] Rather than providing a sense of certainty, the gospel provides clarity of sight.

The remaining three sections dig deeper into the good news of God and how the gospel helps us see and live faithfully. Part 2 explores God's gift of Jesus to the world, what it means to be fully human and alive, and how Jesus spread the good news of peace to a violence-addicted people. Part 3 looks at God's gift of shalom for the common good of all people, and how global peace is deeply intertwined with the welfare of the communities we live in. Part 4 celebrates God's gift of restoring justice and our role as partners in bringing God's kingdom on earth as it is in heaven.

If I were reading a book like this, I might start paging around for a handy how-to guide—you know, ten easy steps to faithfulness. Forty days of something. But that kind of simple manual just doesn't exist, and no good publisher should tell you it does. Becoming a disciple of Christ isn't a single choice we make that can be reduced to an easy plan; it is a lifelong commitment filled with a thousand tiny choices. The more I minister to people passionate about following Jesus right where they are, the more I'm convinced the church needs a new way of making disciples.

So instead of simplistic lists with items to check off, we will look at four core habits—practices that may lead us into new ways of following Jesus right where we are. In each of the four parts of this book, we'll explore one practice, which is more like a new way of being than a subject to study. I believe our discipleship will be energized when we cultivate spiritual imagination in our local community (part 1). Christians will experience

---

1 *Clarify* is a verb with synonyms such as *sheds light on, elucidates, illuminates, enlightens, causes to understand,* and *opens up.* Antonyms include *poor sight, conceal, hide,* and *blindness.*

greater levels of personal transformation with a new disciple-making culture (part 2). Our eyes will be more closely aligned with God's when we read the Bible with voices that are not in the mainstream (part 3). And foundational to our call to follow Jesus in our neighborhoods is orienting ourselves over and over again in worship to the God of mission and justice (part 4).

Faithful living today is rooted in these four spiritual practices, which form us to become the kind of people who naturally love, and which are inspiring faithful witness in communities like yours.

THIS IS NOT A STORY ABOUT ME

I've lived most of my human life thinking I am the main character in my story.

I wish I could tell you that your faith will make you a better lead character in the story of your life. But it's not true. At least not how you might think. Following Jesus has done anything but make me be a better leading man.

Why? Because this is not a story about me! It never has been. I'm not the main character in a story about me. I'm not even a supporting character in a story about me. Not because I'm not up to the challenge (I'm not), but because it's not my story. Why, oh why would I want the story to be about Marty: creator of chaos, redeemer of coupons, king of arrogance, and prince of boredom—when it can be about Jesus: Creator of the Universe, Redeemer of all things, and Prince of Peace in God's kingdom of shalom?

The gospel is helping me find my place in the world as a man who is fearfully and wonderfully made, created a little lower than the angels and crowned with honor. Because the story I'm living is about Jesus, I can tell you without shame that the depression and mood disorder I struggle with are just one part of who

I am, like being right-handed and male. These struggles have taught me how to bring all of who I am to all I know of God—a healing course correction for my theology. And these limits have taught me compassion no sermon ever could—compassion for those I'm called to love *and* compassion for myself.

It has also meant that at times in my life, I've had to follow Jesus into a therapist's office or into line at my local Walgreens pharmacy—because human health matters. I find myself needing to learn that lesson repeatedly. This isn't merely a comment on my personal health; it's tied directly to ministry, and more specifically to my capacity to see clearly. Am I able and willing to see myself as God does? Do I or don't I have gifts to offer my world? Am I part of God's light in the world *despite* or *because of* my vulnerabilities?

We are invited to enter a new story much bigger than our own, the story of God at work in our world. Cosmic and eternal in scope, this story is about the restoration of all creation: things in heaven and things on earth. This is a whole lot bigger than the story I could ever imagine.

I'm thinking of epic stories of people like Esther, who stood up to political bullies, and like William Lawson, whose sixty-year ministry has changed the racial landscape in Houston. Neither of them chose to live in a time of crisis. As Gandalf counsels Frodo in *The Fellowship of the Ring* before Frodo marches toward Mordor, "All we have to decide is what to do with the time that is given us."[2]

It is my deepest prayer that in seeing God more clearly, you'll become a partner in God's amazing peace project right where you already are. Because that's what our communities need: disciples filled with hope and formed by the gospel of Jesus Christ.

---

2 J. R. R. Tolkien, *The Fellowship of the Ring* (New York: Random House, 1954), 56.

Along the way we'll discover a surprising and ancient truth: that the way of living and loving Jesus invites us to *is* the abundant life promised. God, even now and even here, is "able to accomplish abundantly far more than all we can ask or imagine" (Ephesians 3:20).

This is our faith.

This is our hope.

Part I

The Gospel as Lens

*A problem well stated is
a problem half solved.*

—CHARLES KETTERING

ONE

How Jesus' Gospel Clarifies Pretty Much Everything

I LOVE MY CITY, as perhaps you do yours, with a kind of surprising and unchosen affection.

I love Houston, Texas. I love our ridiculously hubristic skyline, our underperforming sports teams, our gargantuan flyovers and twenty-lane highways, our amazing community radio, our plethora of farmers markets, and our longing to be a "real" city—whatever that means. I love our bayous and museums, and all the concerts and shows that cost attendees absolutely nothing. I love our food. In my neighborhood alone you can find excellent Thai, Polish, Mexican, Korean, Vietnamese, and Salvadoran food. I walk with my family to a little churro booth that holds its own against any confection your state fair could ever dream up.

And I love our people—oh, what beautiful and different people we have! An early memory from our move to Houston is taking my family to a play area at Memorial City Mall where children spoke no less than eight languages, confirming how right our move to Houston had been.

But these traits are not *why* I love Houston. In and of themselves, they're simply unable to contain the surprise or affection I feel.

No, I love my city because Houston—no more or less than Pittsburgh, Paducah, or Phnom Penh—is the place that God loves.

It is *a* place, *a* people, *a* city. God's affection is for us; a group of folks trying our best to live in human community. Just as what John taught, saying God loves "the world": our world, our singular world, our one and only God-breathed world.

This continues to astonish me—that God's passion for human flourishing is so limitless that every schoolroom, street, and relationship I've ever had or will have is in the care of God. Everywhere, everything, every time, everyone . . . every, every, every.

God's transformative work ripples out into every arena of human life, from soul to street and every system. As the Dutch theologian Abraham Kuyper said, "There is not a square inch in the whole domain of our human existence over which Christ, who is sovereign over *all*, does not cry: 'Mine!'"[1]

Truly loving Houston—or any place, for that matter—happens not by comparing it to other cities or by longing for a bygone golden age but by seeing my community as God does.

DIAGNOSING REALITY WELL

How exactly does God see our communities? What does God make of a place that was once home to generations of native Karankawa peoples and is now home to six million citizens of a global superpower? How are we doing? How close are we to

---

1 Abraham Kuyper, quoted in William Romanowski, *Eyes Wide Open: Looking for God in Popular Culture* (Grand Rapids: Brazos Press, 2007), 52.

God's intended design—or are we in another turn-the-world-upside-down moment?

And what exactly does it mean that God loves our communities? Is God a tough-love parent, a jealous lover, a fascinated builder?

The biblical authors address these questions repeatedly, using events from the past to help them interpret their own reality. One helpful example of this is how different authors talk about life in the empires of their day. For instance, Egypt was a major power in the region and at times is remembered as a great place for refugees, a place where life can flourish (see the stories of Abraham, Jacob's family, and Jesus' family after his birth).

But that's not all Egypt is. The book of Exodus tells a different story, the horrifying story of enslavement, oppression, and forced labor. Here empire is an evil to be liberated from, a force in the world so bankrupt that God responds with overwhelming power to the cry of the people.

Interpreting their situation as one of oppression led the people of God to very particular, story-specific behavior. They did not at any point try to solve this problem by converting an ever-increasing number of individuals to reach a tipping point toward culture change. They never talked to Pharaoh, to the captain of the guard, or even to Pharaoh's daughter, who raised Moses, to try to convert people in positions of power.

In the same way, Little Rock's Central High School wasn't integrated in 1957 over coffee with Governor Faubus. Nor was the Voting Rights Act passed behind closed doors with President Johnson. Diagnosing a uniquely *cultural* problem required a uniquely *cultural* response.

Now imagine a community, in a particular setting, with real felt needs. Which story of Egypt should they tell? Wouldn't it depend on which cultural understanding made the most sense for their experience? Choosing to tell refugee stories about Egypt might be a great way to give meaning to being a migrant in a strange and benevolent land. Doing so would be an affirmation of current reality. In a different setting, however, telling the exodus story about Egypt might become a rallying cry for citizens to stand strong against oppression and mobilize regime change. "No taxation without representation!" was the cry of the Boston colonists pushing for independence from British rule. Isn't using this Egypt story a decisive protest against the status quo, a cry to God to again liberate people from oppression?

The Chin Emmanuel Church in Houston's Chinatown is filled with refugees escaping terrible violence in their home country of Myanmar. Simon, their pastor, talks about how he has used these two Egypt stories at different times in his people's journey. While they were still in Myanmar, the exodus story proved life-giving, and it is what ultimately led them to their exodus to America and to Anabaptism as a new faith home. Now, as residents in a foreign land, they find that the Bible's Egypt stories also illuminate life in the United States.

If stories of Egyptian empire illustrate God's passion for justice at the national level, empires such as Israel, Babylon, and Rome illuminate God's passion for a new alternative to empire altogether.

This seems to be the lens God uses to interpret the facts on the ground: Are things going well or aren't they? Is it time for a slight course correction? Or are things so rotten it's time to hit the reset button? The flood and Babel and even the destruction of Jerusalem are giant reset buttons: the flood because of violence (Genesis 6:11), Babel for misplaced faith (Genesis 11:6), and Jerusalem due to people's complete lack of community justice (Jeremiah 7:1-15).

There are also overwhelming times of affirmation from God, as when God's people are called to "be fruitful and multiply" (Genesis 1:28) and later to "seek the welfare of the city where I have sent you into exile" (Jeremiah 29:7). Queens like Esther and leaders like Daniel commit their gifts not to revolution but to the common good of their host community. They live faithful lives as refugees and citizens, foreigners and friends in a land that is ultimately not their own.

Every culture and community is filled with both blessing and curse, rich gifts and the potential for harm. The biblical witness clarifies that human communities have been created in goodness, have fallen in fundamental ways, and are being restored.

But the sharpest, most compelling, and passion-filled theology of culture is saved for the New Testament. With the arrival of good news, God's alternative kingdom has come into the heart of the death-dealing Roman Empire.

Rome's empire terrorizes its way to a twisted version of "peace" and the common good. The Jesus kingdom is built on the Christlikeness of a God who is restoring all things through the gospel of peace.

The question comes into sharp focus when Jesus enters the story. Whose kingdom is good news, and whose gospel do you choose?

The story of Jesus' death and resurrection is the early church's clear answer to this question. The first part of the story (his death) unmasks violence for what it is. The latter part (his resurrection) affirms the alternative of God's kingdom.

These analyses are the foundation for relationship between the church and the context in which we find ourselves. Issues of Christian identity and mission, boundaries and purity, and being "in the world but not of it" are all rooted in social analysis.

This relationship between the church and the local community is at the heart of God's mission in our world.

Suffice to say, the Bible is filled with multiple theologies that interpret culture and cities and citizenship. We have to understand our current context to know the path of faithful Christian living. And if we're passionate about making progress toward God's intended design, understanding our context is a great first step.

GOSPEL AS LENS

So are we survivors in a dystopian world or heirs of the stunning gifts of Western civilization—or both at the same time? Is our life as good as it gets, or is another life possible? What *is* the state of the union and the state of every human heart?

To find out, we could turn left and we could turn right; we could ride donkeys or elephants; we could look inward or to the past; we could carve an answer out of personal preference or the dollar signs in our eyes. We could be fair and balanced. We could let Ottawa or Washington decide for us. Every lens we could choose would give us a different answer. Whether by intention or by accident, wearing different lenses would change the way we behave.

But nothing else—not liberalism, conservatism, progressivism, Marxism, capitalism, the scientific method, nor Disney—has the potency to help us understand human existence like the gospel of Jesus the Christ from Nazareth. God's great dreams for personhood and public life as seen in the gospel help us see how far this journey can take us, and how desperately we need the journey.

Here's another way of thinking about how the gospel brings clarity. Imagine being a first responder on the scene of a mass emergency. You must quickly and with some level of precision analyze each case before you. *Triage* is the word for quickly sorting, understanding, and prioritizing what lies before you. Only after triaging patients would you be able to act appropriately in each different and unique case.

In his bestselling book *Blink*, Malcolm Gladwell tells the story of the nation's largest public hospital dramatically improving its triage for potential heart attack patients. Initially the hospital was nearly as likely to mistakenly send a patient home as it was to mistakenly keep them overnight. Short on staff and funds, and swimming with potentially life-threatening cases, the hospital created a simplified diagnostic tool.

Chair of medicine Brendan Reilly began to use four basic observations to determine treatment. It didn't seem likely that narrowing the diagnostic assessments down to four could actually *improve* hospital care. And yet that is exactly what Reilly found to be true.

He found that "what screws up doctors when they are trying to predict heart attacks is that they take too much information into account."[2] Less is more when it comes to rapid assessment for heart issues, with a simple algorithm proving more accurate, efficient, and cost effective than a battery of tests and consultations. Reilly's algorithm proved over time to be accurate for 95 percent of heart patients, while doctors using the traditional method of diagnosis were correct 75–89 percent of the time. Reilly's method has become the new normal for the doctors of Cook County Hospital in Chicago, Illinois.

Has too much information ever slowed down your desire to put faith into action? It certainly can happen, with committees spinning their wheels, churches waiting for more information, and small groups getting all their ducks in a row before moving forward.

---

2 Malcolm Gladwell, *Blink: The Power of Thinking without Thinking* (New York: Little, Brown, 2007), 236.

Take Jesus' teaching that we are to love the hungry, poor, naked, sick, migrants, and prisoners among us. It's possible that before we ever lay eyes on anyone, we get bogged down in conversations about the migrants' documentation, the poor man's work ethic, or the guilt of the imprisoned. Our lists of pros and cons and concern for funding might prove to be too much—too many tests and consultations that lengthen the gap between diagnosis and treatment.

The issues and brokenness of modern life sometimes leave me feeling like that. There are times I just don't understand what is staring me in the face, or *too much* is staring me in the face and I become paralyzed. But what if questions like these weren't answered by complex debates and endless lists of priorities? What if the gospel could triage crucial needs like these in the blink of an eye?

- Why do some schools habitually fail to equip their students, while others do exceptionally well?

- Does loving my neighbor mean supporting Black Lives Matter or "all lives matter"?

- Is immigration a question of hospitality or legality?

- Are the poor lazy, or is there something other than the poor that makes the poor *poor*?

- What effect does endless war have on my community and planet?

- Why are some people's lives stable and wholesome when others' are afflicted and broken?

Evangelical pastor Brian Zahnd finds his simple algorithm in Jesus' theology: "I remember telling my church eight years ago that seeing the kingdom of God had given me 'new eyes.' Reading the Bible with 'kingdom eyes' made scripture brand new to me."[3] Kingdom eyes—gospel eyes—certainly prove more accurate when we encounter the strangers far away and the neighbors near at hand. Because we look with gospel glasses, we'll know what to do.

Steven taught me this lesson in the span of one heartbeat. He had come to our church four Sundays in a row. Each time wanting to kill himself. Each time laden with so much negative emotion he stayed in our parking lot. Finally, on his fifth Sunday, he entered the sanctuary looking for one thing, and one thing only: something to live for. He walked up to me after the service and handed me a bullet, saying, "You can have this. I won't need it anymore."

Was Steven having a spiritual crisis or a human crisis? Wouldn't the gospel say yes to both? Wasn't Steven's life, like those of all people desiring to die by suicide, both broken *and* lost? His was a spiritual crisis of an empty God-shaped hole in his soul, fueled by the devastating human crisis of lacking a gospel-formed community of grace and truth. And nothing short of total human flourishing would meet Steven's deepest needs.

The gospel is why Harriet Tubman (herself suffering from acute vision impairment) saw herself not as a slave victim deserving safety but as a Moses and brave conductor on the Underground Railroad. The gospel is why our schools are integrated and why the church in Houston is leading the campaign against human trafficking, wage theft, and unjust executions. There's nothing that isn't made more clear when viewed through a gospel lens.

The gospel next door is why the saints in history are, well, saints. They're saints because they saw reality *differently.*

3 Brian Zahnd, *A Farewell to Mars: An Evangelical Pastor's Journey toward the Biblical Gospel of Peace* (Colorado Springs: David C. Cook, 2014), 154.

Rosa Parks saw an opportunity where others saw an unbending line not to be crossed. Canadian James Loney—a Christian Peacemaker Teams member held hostage in Iraq in 2006—saw an opportunity to forgive his captors and not seek the death penalty even though they killed fellow hostage Tom Fox.

Clear theological sight is why Dietrich Bonhoeffer and the Confessing Church in Germany named Nazism as evil while others collaborated in the daily, menial, and socially acceptable task of genocide.

And, for regular folks like you and me, the gospel is what helps us know what in the world to think about the stunningly complex events of daily life, from police brutality in our cities to new migrants in our neighborhood to why we still can't break our patterns of unhealthy behavior.

More than anything, clarity of sight helps us to see what God is doing so we can participate both locally and planetwide. The gospel helps us see that it is the church, uniquely located at the hinge of the divine and human, that is the hope of the world. Effective ministry is always squarely rooted in good theology. Without good theology, good behavior is impossible.

All of this raises a pretty important question for us: What on earth is the gospel, anyway?

WHAT ON EARTH IS THE GOSPEL, ANYWAY?

Let's not make that question harder than it needs to be. Jesus' answer was clear and filled with wonder, coming fast on the heels of his commission from God: "The time is fulfilled, and the kingdom of God has come near; repent, and believe in the good news" (Mark 1:15). It is this news—this *good* news about who God is and how God shows up in our world—that uncovers God's intent for our world.

When asked for his agenda, Jesus quickly placed himself in the Spirit's prophetic movement of good news for the poor and captive, for those without healthcare or resources. Having done so, Jesus seems to invite us to come and do likewise.

> The Spirit of the Lord is upon me,
>   because he has anointed me
>   to bring good news to the poor.
> He has sent me to proclaim release to the captives
>   and recovery of sight to the blind,
>   to let the oppressed go free,
> to proclaim the year of the Lord's favor. (Luke 4:18-19)

Later, Jesus pulls us into the place of prayer, where hearts are stirred and imaginations redeemed. In this place he gives us a metaphor rich with life: "Your kingdom come. Your will be done, on earth as it is in heaven" (Matthew 6:10). With this bold prayer we embrace God's intentions for our world and God's great project of restoration.

For Jews like Jesus, the phrase "kingdom of God" wasn't code for the afterlife or God's preferential option for the soul, as if "kingdom of God" and "getting into heaven" were synonyms. For Jews in Jesus' day (and therefore also for Jesus), "kingdom of God" referred to the time of God's rule and reign that would reveal clearly who and how God is. They believed it would arrive through the person and work of a Messiah. It's a robust, earthy concept with political, economic, and spiritual values. The Hebrew worldview didn't allow them to pick and choose from the spiritual and the earthly, like so many choices at a buffet. It's all part of God's gift to humanity.

The rest of the Lord's Prayer is commentary on the kingdom: bread for everyone, freedom from crippling debt and temptation, forgiveness, and detachment from the chaos and evil in our world. God's coming and present kingdom is rooted in our imagination and in the grand vision that the cities we live in and the neighborhoods we inhabit are being re-created to reflect heaven itself.

I wonder if Jesus knew that the only way we'd understand the gospel would be if he bypassed our minds and their addiction to productivity and went straight to our hearts. After all, Martin Luther King Jr. didn't energize a movement by saying, "I have a plan!"

With words of prayer—whether uttered by Jesus' lips or our own—we're invited to enter a new reality: the story of God at work in our world. Cosmic and eternal in scope, this story is about the restoration of all creation: things in heaven and things on earth. That's a whole lot bigger than the things I've often made my own life story about: getting the girl, living a safe suburban life, being competent.

The early church experienced the gospel in nearly every area of life imaginable. They connected the gospel to God, Jesus, the kingdom of God, peace, creation, grace, forgiveness, salvation, reconciliation, healing, calling, mystery, the broadening of salvation to Gentiles, promises fulfilled, and the complete story of Jesus' life.

The audience to which the gospel is directed includes all people, all creation, those who believe, Jews and Gentiles alike. It seems to be especially given to the most vulnerable among us. And, for the New Testament authors, the gospel wasn't merely about receiving from God; it was a holistic experience that transformed their ideas and actions. The gospel transforms us to witness, work, evangelize, proclaim, suffer, participate in its growth and spread, and—perhaps most of all—follow Jesus. These lists about the content, audience, and action of the gospel are impressive!

The gospel is about far more than *me* or *you*. It is about far more than forgiveness of personal sins and connection to the afterlife. It's about who—and how—God is in places like Houston on a daily basis. It is about the goodness of divine activity experienced most potently in Jesus the Christ. God is passionate about addressing both spiritual and physical starvation, and about bridging the gap between the world as it is and the world as it can be.

God is restoring all things, and when the New Testament writers say "all," they mean *all*—as in "all things, whether on earth or in heaven" (Colossians 1:20). This is why the early church imagined Jesus' *entire* story as gospel: from his early beginnings as a poor refugee and his acceptance of social outcasts to his execution, which unmasked violence as morally bankrupt.

Indeed, the one irreducible gospel truth that shapes and reshapes the church is that God's love is not limited—not to souls or eternal reward, not to bodies or politics, not to human or divine relationships. God's love is for the world and everything in it. Thankfully, that includes you and me!

The culture of the gospel itself reveals who and how God is. It's quite appropriate, in this broad sense, to call the gospel the good news about our good God's good acts in our good world. News about such a God is good precisely because it is a story about the here-and-now acts of God in Christ to restore wholeness—a journey that spans time into all eternity.

The incarnational gift of Jesus is such a limitless gift that Paul says God who is "at work within us is able to accomplish abundantly far more than all we can ask or imagine" (Ephesians 3:20). Gospel is good news for all life. Neither personal salvation nor political liberation is a large enough container to hold all the goodness of God.

When we see the world through the eyes of God and not our own, practicing our faith comes into greater focus. Embracing the gospel as good news for all life helps us respond to the physical and spiritual hunger around us.

TWO

Borrowing the Eyes
of God

BOB AND CATHIE Baldwin have eyes to see what others have not.

They have been longtime neighbors of a mobile home park. They've seen families quickly come and go, and they've watched the park's ownership change hands almost as fast. Families have cycled in and out based on the cycles of poverty they were stuck in; owners have cycled in and out with an eye to the bottom line of profit.

Over time the park's infrastructure deteriorated, as did the character of the residents. For most area neighbors, this was a pretty simple situation. The park was a problem, the people were a problem, and problems like this are solved by organizing against the problem-makers. And organize they did, using all their wealth and connections to shut down the park altogether. While most of these organized neighbors were church members, they never asked whether the current mobile home park owner was a Christian or whether the residents were sisters and brothers in Christ. They never really saw the owner or residents as neighbors at all, perhaps because residents were largely undocumented immigrants.

One day as Bob walked past the park he had never once set foot in, he heard a surprising and seemingly divine invitation that would change him forever: "If you don't like the way this park is being run, why don't you run it?" Soon thereafter Bob learned that the owner was worshiping at the same church he did. It was a church the Baldwins had joined specifically to teach what it means to follow Jesus where we live, work, and play.

Slowly God began to change the Baldwins' way of looking at their neighbors. Yes, there was a problem, but not in the same way others thought. The problem wasn't the people or the park; it was how disconnected they were from their immediate community and from resources that could help residents flourish. The problem wasn't their wealthy neighbors' irritation; it was the plight of the people.

The Baldwins began to believe that what residents in the park needed wasn't a good talking-to; it was a loving owner invested in the community with dignity and care. Instead of working to shut the park's gate, they purchased the park themselves. They made a commitment to the people who lived there that they would do all they could to build the common good.

They began making extensive upgrades in relationships and facilities, added a park and community center, and started programs for the children and English and computer classes for adults. They hired from among the residents whenever possible and made themselves readily available to residents for any needs that arose. Foremost on their hearts was how they could be the church to these people and demonstrate an alternative kingdom way of living.

Can you imagine everything that changed when the Baldwins began to see their neighborhood with different eyes? Certainly the lives of their tenants and their sense of community changed. And the neighbors of the mobile home park changed their perceptions as well, perhaps finding some release from their anxiety about a people different from themselves. The Baldwins' commitment to the common good of their neighborhood has since spilled well beyond their mobile home park to include their wider community. When a brand-new housing development went up across from the mobile home park, the Baldwins realized with sadness there were no plans for any shared, common space, which is essential for the flourishing of any human community. So they donated land for an outdoor common space for the new residents, believing that all neighborhoods need space for relationships to form and take shape.

For the Baldwins' part, treating people how they would want neighbors to treat them turned out to be a great business decision. Not only have they given much; they've been given much in return. But the real change may be in Bob himself, whose faith flourished when he joined God on mission in this way. Bob was changed because he came to realize that the abundant life promised is a life lived in love of his neighbors.

And it all started by borrowing the eyes of God.

WHAT IS GOD DOING, ANYWAY?

If the blame and praise heaped on Jesus tells us anything, it's that this is easier said than done. Apparently Jesus is either a walking heretic or a hero; it all depends on whether you believe him. Not believe *in* him, but *believe* him—as in, take him at his word that his is the best way to live. And no matter how oblivious our biased faith makes us, the characters in the Gospels got it wrong as often as right.

So how can Jesus—seen either as a hero or as a heretic—clarify for us the kind of things we'll see when we watch God working in our world?

John makes this lesson easy for us in his gospel. If you want to see God, look at Jesus.

It's a pretty basic equation, really. Jesus says it like this, "The Son can do nothing on his own, but only what he sees the Father doing. . . . The Father loves the Son and shows him all that he himself is doing" (John 5:19-20). Jesus claims, in no uncertain terms, that he only does what he sees God doing. That's it, period. Nothing more, nothing less.

Somehow, some way, Jesus watched God and chose to do the same things in the same way. This shouldn't be any surprise to us. Our children watch us to know what to do and mimic us without even knowing it. Sometimes this is good, and sometimes it gets a bit embarrassing. The same is true when keeping up with the Joneses, or learning a sport, or understanding a new job.

We *can* see who and how God is in our world, and we do so most clearly through Jesus, whose lifestyle mimicked God. Jesus claimed he both saw and heard from God and never acted on his own will: "I seek to do not my own will but the will of him who sent me" (John 5:30); "I declare what I have seen in the Father's presence; as for you, you should do what you have heard from the Father" (John 8:38).

Over and over, John makes it clear. Abraham, Moses, or a flat reading of Scripture is not Jesus' model for behavior: God alone is. Jesus saw the world through the eyes of God and mimicked what he saw God doing.

What difference does good theology make anyway? Does it make any difference in how I should vote next week or in how I treat my coworkers tomorrow? Consider the way you might act if your image of God (either unconsciously or intentionally) was a distant, demanding parent, or how your behavior might differ if your God was a candy-store God who gave you everything you've ever wanted. If you think God just kept humming away, unmoved on 9/11 while three thousand people died, we could hardly fault you for tackling your community's deepest needs by yourself. If God resents creation and can't wait to destroy it, or demands payment for sin so strongly he willingly abuses his own Son, might that not change how you think of God and how you behave?

Personally, my image of God has been so deeply tied to how my parents repeatedly rescued me that I lived with a debilitating sense of entitlement for decades. What freedom it is to encounter a God who believes I have everything I already need for life and godliness.

But what if God were like Jesus? What if God were deeply engaged, extravagantly loving, passionately communal, infinitely absorbing of hate, and radically local? That would change everything, wouldn't it?

Jesus invited us to love God with all our being, so we better get this right. We've also been asked to love one another the way Jesus loves us—so we definitely better get this right!

Good theology matters. It matters when we have crucial conversations about our beliefs and practices as a church. It matters when we think about our own potential for goodness in the world. And it matters when we pray and gather for worship.

Vision—seeing clearly, perceiving, understanding, grasping, comprehending, hearing, and obeying the actions of God—is a core theme throughout John's gospel.[1] John is teaching us to see. And for John, the clear answer to the question of how we know what God does in the world is that we watch Jesus live.

---

1 See John 3:3; 5:19, 30; 7:16; 8.26, 28, 40, 9.4, 12:49-50; 14:9, 31; 15:15; 16:13; 17:26.

In fact, John's gospel reads like a diagnostic manual for spiritual blindness. He's like an eye doctor doing an exam: "Read the smallest line you can see on this chart. You can't see any of the letters? Maybe it's time you considered surgery."

God is at work in our world, doing the very things we see *Jesus* doing in the Gospels. Which is what, exactly?

This is where it gets interesting.

MIND THE GAP

Where successful men see business opportunities, Jesus sees tables to throw around. Where some see an impassable border, Jesus sees a gospel doorway. Enemies are no more, rules can be broken, and true faithfulness takes the curious path of downward mobility. *Surprise!*

Jesus charges in when tensions are high and violence is expected, standing in the gap between people in conflict. Everything and everyone—every sinner and Sabbath law—Jesus sees completely differently from the way others do. Too often we get caught thinking some people are sinners and others saints; we see some rules as sacrosanct and others as able to be interpreted away. But Jesus looked with God's eyes, and he saw a widening integrity gap between the way things are and the way God intended them to be. Both sides in a conflict struggle with spiritual desolation; both are caught in institutions that can themselves be morally bankrupt.

All this would be bizarre if it weren't so beautiful.

For it is here in the gap where God is moving, restoring all things to their original design. And nothing clarifies the gaps like the holistic gospel of Jesus. Writing in the midst of German warfare, German theologian Karl Barth translates Romans 12:2 with gospel critique in mind. He suggests that Paul urges us "not to fashion yourselves according to the present form of this world, but according to its coming transformation, by renewing your mind."[2]

Where people fall short of the abundant life promised, God is there in the gap. When the common good fails to feed hungry mouths in our school classrooms, God is there in the gap. Between the gospel's intentions and current reality is the heart of Christian living, for it is where gospel and culture intersect that the mission of the church is born. How can the church become a gospel-formed culture that enters these gaps?

Like a movie trailer put out weeks before a movie is released, the church is a glimpse for the watching world of all that God intends for human flourishing. We live today as if the kingdom were already here. We live it, embrace it, imagine it, and defend it. We ask ourselves what people and communities will look like when they're fully functioning as God designed, and we live that way today. We call out the lies of the world that are counter to the kingdom of God and boldly spread the news that a new world is coming and is already here.

The mission of the church isn't just about *where* we live but also the *way* we live. The transformative message of God's kingdom has forever and henceforth been embodied in human flesh. Billboards, sermons, tweets, and podcasts only hint at the depth of the gospel of God.

Only flesh can demonstrate the gospel—only flesh infused with Spirit, with love, with the character and behavior of Jesus Christ, fully human and perfectly revealing how God is in our world. In the shared lives of Christ's followers in the church, we demonstrate the lifestyle of Jesus before the watching world.

We are part of the gospel message itself. The distinct quality and character of the church is that we are the body of *Christ*. We're not just any ol' body; we're representatives of Jesus and

2 Karl Barth, *The Epistle to the Romans* (New York: Oxford University Press, 1950), 424.

of his way of life. Jesus consistently places at the core of his mission our organic togetherness. He says we're the light of the world together—*you*, plural—not as individuals trying to change the course of history.

The very essence of Jesus' teachings is love. Love as reconciliation, love as forgiveness, love as restoring community and shalom, love as peace breaking down walls that divide. A people who love God, self, others, and our enemies: this is the kind of gospel-formed community that Jesus was forming. This is the incarnational community that God sends into the world.

That the medium (church) is part of the message (gospel) cuts directly through debates about whether Christian faith is about the personal or the social, Jesus or justice. No! It's all that and more. God's love for the world includes all hearts, all organizations, and all cultures of people everywhere.

We—as in you and I—are partners in God's peace project right where we are. Mission isn't for special people called "missionaries" doing special things called "missions" in special places such as some far-off mission field. We are called to do the kinds of things Jesus would do if he were living our lives.

EYEWITNESS NEWS

In late 2012, I began to understand God's mission as the closing of gaps, and to see God present in the gaps around me. I'd witnessed changes in my own heart and heard stories like that of the Baldwins, and I wanted to give testimony to what I had seen. Psalm 145 became my template: "Your majesty and glorious splendor *have captivated me*; I will meditate on Your wonders, *sing songs of Your worth*. We confess—there is *nothing greater than You, God,* nothing mightier than Your awesome works. I will tell of Your greatness *as long as I have breath*" (Psalm 145:5-6 The Voice).

I believed then as I do now that I've seen God's liberating presence, and I want to give witness.

I think this is what the gospel authors were doing as well: giving testimony by pointing to what they'd seen Jesus doing. But they also tell a different story about how stunningly wrong so many eyewitnesses got it. Maybe that shouldn't surprise us.

Remember all the times Jesus did some stunning act of gospel (healing, eating at all the wrong tables, disarming a mob, forgiving sins), only to be misinterpreted as working for the devil, or Beelzebub, or whomever the enemy happened to be?

Take, for instance, Jesus' visit to the Bethesda pools in John 5. On a fine Sabbath day, Jesus met a man who was utterly alone and outcast in every sense of the word. He had been ill for thirty-eight years, and so, in a subversive act of dignity, Jesus healed the man. "'Take your mat and walk.' At once the man was made well, and he took up his mat and began to walk" (John 5:8-9).

This is an incredible God story, isn't it? It is a clear example of who and how God is in our world: healing, restoration of wholeness, a man's first chance to connect meaningfully with his community and worship legally in his temple and find dignified work to support himself. Grab the mic, this man's got a testimony!

So why did the eyewitnesses not see that? They questioned, prodded, interrogated, and eventually persecuted Jesus for what we see as obvious but they saw as dangerous. They "started persecuting Jesus, because he was doing such things on the sabbath" (John 5:16). They obviously didn't see God working in Jesus.

Even so, I can't help but see myself in these leaders. What strikes me isn't that they appear to be out to sabotage Jesus. What strikes me is how faithful and committed they were—to

God, Scripture, tradition, and faith—in the best ways their religion allowed. They believed, as I might have in their shoes, that Scripture was not to be bent, let alone dismissed. It was literal, universal, and true.

It appears that they were wrong not despite their faithfulness but *because* of it. What they thought God should be doing and what he was actually doing were two completely different things. They missed seeing God altogether, and their behavior showed it.

Soon they were not only persecuting Jesus but also actively working to kill him. They were completely unable to place the spiritual desolation of one hurting man over their unwavering commitment to accepted scriptural norms. For these witnesses, it was quite clear: the wrong man was working the wrong deed on the wrong day for the wrong reasons.

Before you dismiss the religious leaders for being on the wrong side of history, let's not forget Jesus had to keep teaching this to his closest followers, including Peter, who needed repeated visions to dismantle his blindness. It seems unlikely that Jesus confronted the spiritual leaders of his day in order to support the religious leaders of ours.

BAND-AIDS ON BULLET HOLES

Without struggling to overcome our own blind spots, we're destined to lead unfaithful—and sometimes downright dangerous—Christian lives.

One of the worst mistakes the church can make is misdiagnosis. Sometimes we've misinterpreted the oppression of Egypt as exile in Babylon, and instead of seeking revolutionary liberation, we've pursued cultural assimilation. With good intentions and full commitment to certain Christian values, the church has misdiagnosed the brokenness, which has led repeatedly to ineffective solutions. It's a bit like putting Band-Aids on bullet wounds. An improper diagnosis leads inevitably to improper behavior.

When we don't understand the spiritual needs of individuals or our culture, it makes it difficult to respond faithfully. Blindness forces us to mistake piety (personal relationship with God), church membership, and worship as the total requirements of Christian living. Just slip a new Christian soul into your American glove and go about life as you've always lived it.

When my congregation, Houston Mennonite Church, was birthed in 1967, its understanding of its ministry to Houston was typical of the day. We were a place for spiritual nourishment, attracting people who wanted the religious goods we offered. Absent from our DNA was a sense of purpose tying our own spiritual health to the health of our community. We didn't understand our community's needs, or our role in it, or how essential the word *Houston* is to our name. The common good simply wasn't on our radar screen; attracting members was. This is what we knew, and we did the best we could with what we'd inherited.

Jesus does not hesitate to tell us quite plainly when our perception of the world has led to unfaithful practice. At one point he confronted a group who must have assumed the status quo was working well enough and only needed occasional acts of charity to fill in small gaps. But Jesus was not content with the status quo and realized deeper changes than charity were needed. "So woe to you, teachers of the law and Pharisees. You hypocrites! You tithe from *your luxuries and your spices, giving away a tenth of* your mint, your dill, and your cumin. But you have ignored the essentials of the law: justice, mercy, faithfulness. It is practice of the latter that makes sense of the former" (Matthew 23.23 The Voice).

A worldview unable to identify the gaps is unable to equip us for faithful discipleship today.

Blindness to the gaps creates religion that underwrites Western culture. Presidential candidates are forced to proclaim faith in God and war at the same time; border militarization trumps an ethic of hospitality to the stranger; and missionaries can unwittingly export Western culture along with some version of Jesus' message.

Is it possible for the church to form disciples of Jesus while aligned so firmly with the very powers from which we need saving?

Assuming our world has no gaps communicates that being born again is as American as apple pie and that we are a "Christian" nation. Since we're a Christian nation, you just need to take that one final step and give your heart to Jesus; all other practices can remain intact. The gospel becomes a seed planted into an otherwise acceptable cultural soil.

When all is well and the gaps are undiscernible, we may pat ourselves on the back for giving up Friday night hamburgers or Facebook during Lent. A couple of hours of volunteering per month might look pretty radical in a world without need.

But in a world that needs total inversion, those faithful behaviors may prove inadequate to the needs of our community. Looking at the world as Jesus does shows us that a true fast is not forty days without chocolate but a radical commitment of entering the gap for the restoration of all things. As Isaiah says,

> Is not this the fast that I choose:
>   to loose the bonds of injustice,
>   to undo the thongs of the yoke,
> to let the oppressed go free,
>   and to break every yoke?
> Is it not to share your bread with the hungry,
>   and bring the homeless poor into your house;

when you see the naked, to cover them,
    and not to hide yourself from your own kin? (Isaiah 58:6-7)

This is not a fast for those living in the lap of luxury, but for those who look and live like Jesus.

Closer to home, our Christian story is overrun with ways we've gotten it wrong dangerously wrong. Turning people off-from-God wrong.

For centuries, European Christians believed the lie that God was acting on their behalf, helping them colonize the new world. We adopted what's been called the Doctrine of Discovery and lived accordingly, as colonizers able to take land and kill the peoples of the indigenous nations in the name of God. Southern slavery stood on the tall shoulders of Scripture, negating the notion that "All men are created equal." Women have been treated as subhuman and abused thanks to traditional scriptural interpretations. Loving strangers—which once took the shape of "Give me your tired, your poor, your huddled masses"—has long been supplanted by homeland security, militarized borders, and thirty-four thousand noncriminal migrants locked up on any given day in U.S. detention centers.

We miss John's intent in telling stories of Jesus' healing if we see them only as proof of divinity and not as lessons on how to truly see God at work in our world. What is God trying to tell us in these stories? We find God doing the very thing the prophets promised. God cares for our bodies and physical health.

John is teaching us to see!

LOCATION SHAPES MISSION

I think that's why the Baldwins' outreach to their neighbors was so wholesome. They were able to see their location more clearly, which allowed them to respond holistically. They addressed the layers of cultural brokenness by sharing the culture of Christ with all its many layers of healing. Rather than one-to-one ministry, they embodied a new way of being that both demonstrated God's love to their neighbors in the mobile home park and prophetically challenged their wealthy neighbors to see God working in ways wider than they could previously imagine.

Living today how things will ultimately be is fundamental to the church's mission in our world. Missiologist David Bosch says, "Those who know that God will one day wipe away all tears will not accept with resignation the tears of those who suffer and are oppressed *now*. Anyone who knows that one day there will be no more disease can and must actively anticipate the conquest of disease in individuals and society *now*. And anyone who believes that the enemy of God and humans will be vanquished will already oppose him *now* in his machinations in family and society. For all of this has to do with salvation *now*."[3]

In writing *The Gospel Next Door*, I've come to see how radical it can be when we connect biblical imagination with our context. I think this is what the New Testament authors do so well. They localize their writing and give it meaning by rooting it in real-life stories. Sometimes they reference local political leaders or pinpoint a specific city where Jesus' story takes place to remind us how unique the story really is. John brings the story closer to home than any, saying that Jesus' incarnation was a sign that God had "moved into the neighborhood" (John 1:14 *The Message*). For the early church, there was something so essential about context-bound theologizing that they refused to dabble in systemic theology at all.

In a riff on the fourth-century Apostles' Creed, here's some locally grown, 100 percent organic, straight-to-your-table theology for a Houston neighborhood. Maybe it's a neighborhood a lot like yours.

---

3 David Bosch, *Transforming Mission* (Maryknoll, NY: Orbis Books, 1999), 410.

I BELIEVE GOD the Father of others, maker of Houston and its
differences.

I BELIEVE JESUS not Caesar,
Son of the people and model of peace,
who was conceived for ordinary people like Valerie, my neighbor,
born to set human traffickers and their victims free,
he suffers with Black Lives Matter.

He is executed with inmates at the Walls Unit and is buried
with our uninsured dead.
He descends to serve families in the hell of homelessness.
He is raising up the poor and pushed-out—immigrants corralled
in the for-profit Houston Contract Detention Center and lesbian
sisters unwelcome in the church and afraid for their safety.
He ascends to the spiritually famished to sit with them in the
uncomfortable gap between their espoused and their lived
values.
From where he sits, he clearly sees Montrose and Midtown and
Manchester as they are and are meant to be.

I BELIEVE THE SPIRIT is closing those gaps,
through a reborn church that for too long neglected the common
good,
that Christians are bravely gathering together to live as Jesus
taught,
that every street and soul is being restored to its design,
that it's not too late to resurrect old dreams
of equal education for public and private schools,
for the Energy Capital of the World to lead in energy
sustainability,
that we can trade "open carry" for open love of neighbor and
enemy alike.

I BELIEVE IN the eternal life of Christ's kingdom of peace and the
inevitable demise of America's kingdom of war. Amen.

Perhaps this kind of theology will equip missional communities like yours to engage our world faithfully today. Churches are beginning to apply broad truths such as "All people are created in the image of God" to Syrian refugees, immigrants without papers, and the Black Lives Matter movement. We're taking fundamental moral principles like "prolife" and putting them to work in our execution chambers and healthcare policies and abortion clinics. "For God so loved the world" is nudging us to see how our local behavior influences our neighbors near and far.

What are the things you sense God is doing in your neck of the woods? How might localizing your theology strengthen your involvement in God's mission? How does your location shape the way you live your faith?

THREE

Tell Them about the Dream!

TEACUPS. That's artist Robert Hodge's dream for Houston's future, specifically the black youth in Houston. He wants to be able to paint things like teacups, and flowers. "Abstract and pretty, everything's abstract," he said. "I want future black artists to worry about paint, and the nuanced way light hits the canvas. But it's all abstract—abstract, abstract, abstract—and beautiful. I dream of a day when there's no need for art that raises social consciousness. So yeah, I want to paint teacups."

As an African American artist, Robert was part of a panel celebrating and challenging the work of the church in Houston's black community. Freedom dreams like his are as vital as action for faithful followers. Robert is not the only one with dreams. I wonder what you dream for the future of your community.

When Dave Peterson asked the question and it was too late to take back, it felt more playful than prayerful. Dave had sat with area pastors praying for our city dozens of times just like this. But today was different; today he wondered aloud, "What if?"

Houston's reputation was unparalleled in several noteworthy sectors, but it lagged in others. Our schools, in particular, were not functioning as designed or needed, and schools were on Dave's heart as he prayed, "What if we were as well known for our whole and healthy children as we are for being the space city and the energy capital of the world?"

That simple question—what if?—was like rocket fuel, moving them instantly beyond prayerful and playful to prophetic. Dave's imagination became the voice God chose to speak to those in the room.

What if? Has there ever been a question that has so changed the world as this one, uttered in prayerful awe? Seeing the beauty of God's intent for all creation inspires us to move into the gap between the world as it is and as it can be.

PRACTICING OUR SPIRITUAL IMAGINATION

The practice of using a spiritual imagination is the first of four core habits we will look at in this book. It's one that missional communities can embrace in their quest to follow Jesus right where they are. This practice is about our imagination because all Christian practices are intertwined with hope about a story far larger than our own. But it's not about our own hopes and opinions about the way things should be. It's uniquely "spiritual," because it's rooted firmly in the Bible's vision for human flourishing.

As in countless other cities, Christians in Houston have dared to imagine that God is freeing the captives of human trafficking. They've seen in the exodus and exile stories of liberation, in Jesus' teaching and Paul's exorcisms, that God really is about the work of "proclaiming liberty to the captives." And having seen God's action in the story of Scripture, they've dared to dream that God would do it again right where they are.

Erica Raggett was devastated when she first learned her beloved city of Houston was the North American hub of young women being trafficked for sex. This news didn't leave her paralyzed and angry, though. Her church pointed her to what was already happening and to the fact that Houston's churches were leading the way in efforts to overcome this evil.

Seeing the incredible brokenness alongside the powerful stories of church action helped her see that what our city needed most was a different kind of hub for gathering, and A 2nd Cup coffee shop was born. Training, events, fundraisers, and gathering space are all available to those who are working to close the gap between the world as it is and as it was intended to be.

One way Erica's coffee shop does this is so obvious it might be missed: it offers coffee produced without slave labor. "You can't claim to be against modern-day slavery and still drink coffee harvested by slaves," said Erica. She's fighting human trafficking one venti caramel latte at a time. She does it not as a coffee vendor but because she knows she's living an ancient dream fit for today.

Julie Waters, founder of Free the Captives Houston, is a modern-day Harriet Tubman, providing amazing holistic aftercare for women who have been rescued out of slavery. Her volunteers are some of the boldest people I know in Houston. They know where the brothels and the women who need liberation are, offering them exceptional aftercare ministry. They confront men who buy sex and lead the charge to "reduce the demand" for paid sexual services. Julie's ministry, an amazing expression of Jesus' good news, "engages and mobilizes the Christian community and partners with nonprofits, law enforcement, and government agencies in the fight against modern day slavery." That vision, displayed on the ministry's website, has found genuine root in Houston's imagination and church community.

Kingsland Baptist Church in Katy, Texas, has an exceptional "across the street and around the world" approach to what they see God doing to liberate the oppressed. Pastor Omar Garcia leads his congregation in local ministries that educate and rescue local victims, but his church also realizes that in our globalized economy, Houston is connected to slavery in other parts of the world. Thus, the congregation also connects with partners on the ground in Asia to combat violence against women on literally a global scale.

For Christians in Houston who are witnesses of this work, it is a reminder that the neighborhood outside our door is nothing short of the place of God's great mission. This is a truth we can only dare to believe through the gospel of Jesus Christ.

REDEEMING THE IMAGINATION

Mahalia Jackson knew the power of the imagination when she shouted to Martin Luther King Jr. during his 1963 speech at the National Mall in Washington, "Tell them about the dream, Martin!" This electrifying speech energized a movement the moment King spoke to our hearts rather than minds: "I have a dream . . ."

The same can be true of Christians in all places and ages: we can evoke a holy imagination to transform the world and our place in it. Perhaps imagination is even fundamental to our faithfulness.

The prophet Nathan used imagination to transform the heart of King David. Mary sang a song that shaped the inverted worldview of her son Jesus. Isaiah's image of the peaceable kingdom continues to inspire us twenty-six centuries later, with animals turned into friends and weapons into tools. Christian artist and songwriter Michael Card says that "as created beings, one of our greatest treasures—perhaps the dearest fingerprint of God in us—is our ability to imagine."[1]

---

1 Michael Card, *Luke: The Gospel of Amazement* (Downers Grove, IL: InterVarsity Press, 2011), 17.

Paul uses his ability to imagine to dismantle our limited expectations, setting our spirits free to soar: "What no eye has seen, nor ear heard, nor the human heart conceived, what God has prepared for those who love him" (1 Corinthians 2:9).

In other words, *what if?*

Jonah Lehrer, in his book *Imagine*, calls this "trespassing on the realm of the holy." Lehrer suggests, along with the prophets and authors of old, that our most important talent is "the ability to imagine what has never existed. We take this for granted but our lives are defined by it."[2]

Martin Luther King Jr. may have dared to "imagine what has never existed," but he did not conjure it from thin air like the fantastical worlds of Lewis, Dr. Seuss, or Rowling. When he said "I have a dream," he didn't leave us wondering where to find Platform 9¾ like an adolescent Harry Potter.

The dream was birthed not in the mind of one person but in the story of God at work in our world. King's soaring poetry was always rooted in the rock of Scripture.

FREEDOM DREAMS

Missional communities, pastors, and ordinary congregations like yours are being infused with energy through the practice of spiritual imagination. By writing their own "I Have a Dream" speech for their neighborhoods, mission becomes clear. You may not think of yourself as a creative person! But not to worry: I'm not asking you to conjure anything from thin air. I'm asking you to "view the present through the promise," as Thomas Troeger's creative song urges us.

Practice using a spiritual imagination. Try looking at your city through the lens of the gospel—God's preferred future.

---

2 Jonah Lehrer, *Imagine: How Creativity Works* (Boston: Houghton Mifflin Harcourt, 2012), xv.

Take your time, form a small learning group, and press in together with the goal of seeing the world with the eyes of God.

Together learn the story of the place you've been called to and the people who live there.

Take the time to listen well to the stories of how your community was formed and how it has transformed over the years. Tours through a neighborhood with seasoned leaders in faith, business, nonprofit, education, and civic arenas who are able to recount changes over time can prove invaluable. Speak to grandmothers and pastors in minority, immigrant, and poor communities to hear the strengths and brokenness they experience. Simply walking your neighborhood will help you learn about real neighbors God may be calling you to love.

Once you have a better grasp of the neighborhood you want to partner with, explore what it looks like when you take the grand truths of Scripture and drop them into a neighborhood near you.

Here are several concrete practices congregations and missional communities are using to capture God's vision.

- Read Isaiah 65:17-25 by yourself or in a small group. Consider how you might recast this lovely passage for your own ministry and that of your congregation. What might this chapter sound like if Isaiah were writing it today, in your context? The more specific the better.

- Discern together the giants of injustice. Where is there injustice, brokenness, things not working as they should? Where is there what we might call "unpeace": the opposite of God's desires? What institutions are no longer reliably serving the common good? What is creating poverty, healthcare, and criminal justice crises in your area? Who is falling through the service gaps, and why? Who is hiding in the shadows, and why? Who is new in the community, without full access to leadership or institutions?

- Discuss what your congregation's neighborhood would look like if God's will were done in it "as it is in heaven." Be playful and specific. Dream boldly. Diagnose transparently. Pray prophetically.

- Have an Instagram party! Invite everyone in your missional community to bring a picture they've taken of something or someone right outside their door. It can be the door outside your home, business, or favorite restaurant. Ask yourself, what is God doing there, and how can I join in?

- Invite people to complete Martin Luther King Jr.'s powerful sentence, "I have a dream . . ."

- Ask yourselves and people from various sectors what they are most concerned with in their community. What longings do they have for their community? What are they hungry for?

Robert Hodge's dream for painted teacups reminds us of the incredible power of art for social critique. I think of my first encounter with such paintings as *Potato Eaters* by Vincent van Gogh, or *The Scream* by Edvard Munch, or *Guernica* by Pablo Picasso. Each revealed a level of humanity to me I've yet to forget. I remember leading a youth group prayer time the day after the World Trade Center attacks, and how one student painted *The Scream* as her prayer for the night.

The practice I'm inviting you to is this: Connect your context as specifically as you can to the story of Scripture. Move beyond a list of goals and outcomes, and let your heart be captured by the possible.

Here's an example. In a recent retreat with the board and staff of Newspring, a faith-based nonprofit in Houston's Spring Branch neighborhood, I led the participants in the spiritual practice of vision-casting. As part of that retreat, I asked them to rewrite Isaiah 65:17-25 for their own ministry. Here was what Newspring staff person Kristen Gonzalez dreamed:

> Chill out, I got this! I'm making Spring Branch better. I'm paving it with gold and it will be paradise. No person will have a reason to be sad, upset, lonely, or miserable. You will work hard, but you will love your work and you will see your effect and it will bring you joy. You will love everybody and they will love you, you will not hate or dislike, only love.

And so we might ask: What if our churches would imagine our cities as places where God's redemptive justice and shalom flourish—and then conspire accordingly? What if, rather than each congregation functioning as a silo trying to fill its own pews, we would work as the body of Christ?

Redeeming the imagination isn't about selling opinions or pie-in-the-sky whims. Spiritual imagination is always rooted in God's gospel and the restoration of things through Jesus, a marginalized Jew from a backwater town lost in the shadows of empire.

When the church dares to dream, we point forward toward the world as God intended by giving witness to what we've already seen. And what is the world as God intended? This isn't a question we're left on our own to ponder. Though we see it as through an opaque window, the outlines are there to see in the gospel. Let's turn our attention to the gospel—God's good news about human flourishing—to give color and shape to the church's dreams. Jesus, shalom, and restoring justice are at the heart of who and how God chooses to show up in our world.

Part II

The Gospel Gift
of Jesus

I need Christ, not something that resembles Him.

—C. S. LEWIS
A GRIEF OBSERVED

FOUR

Look like Jesus

IN SEPTEMBER 2008, Hurricane Ike slammed into Houston and Galveston, Texas, killing dozens, flooding one hundred thousand homes, and causing $20 billion in damages. Twelve hundred miles away, my wife and I watched the chaos unfold on our television screen. Houston Mennonite Church had just invited me to become their pastor, and I had said yes. Watching the news reports, we couldn't help wondering what on earth we'd gotten ourselves into. On that day, when brokenness and wind swirled, we had no idea how deeply Houston would shape us.

Weeks after moving to Houston, with signs of destruction from the hurricane still around, I met Linda. She had been driving south on Wirt Road where our church building is located. With tears flooding her eyes, making it impossible to see, Linda didn't have any idea where she was, and she pulled into the first parking lot she could find.

Linda pounded on our church door, weeping and desperate for someone, anyone, to answer. I was away from the building, eating lunch with one of our church leaders. With no one to answer her knock, Linda riffled through her car and scrounged up all the money she had. She then laid it all, roughly three dollars, on the stoop of our church's front door as a kind of offering.

"This is all I've got, God!" she wailed. "If you don't save me, I'm done." Kneeling, weeping, and crying out to God, she was in obvious crisis.

That's when I showed up, like a stranger stumbling into the wrong hospital room and catching the occupant half dressed. She assumed that I was an answer to her prayer. I sure didn't feel like an answer to any prayer. Linda's hair was a mess, her makeup was running from tears and saliva, her clothes were scanty and pulled this way and that, and she looked at me with terrified eyes. But it was the bruises I'll never forget. They were everywhere and covered her legs, face, and arms. I didn't know anything about her story, and yet in the blink of an eye, I knew more about her than I've learned about some people I've known most of my lifetime.

It took a full fifteen minutes of me quietly repeating this prayer aloud before she calmed down enough to tell me her story: "Grace to you and peace from God and your brother Jesus. . . . Grace to you and peace from God and your brother Jesus. . . . Grace to you and peace from God and your brother Jesus. . . ."

I learned that Linda was a stripper who had lost her job and was badly beaten when she tried to escape the man who forced her to work against her will. This was years ago, before I had heard of human trafficking. Now, looking back, I know she was a victim, forced to sell sex and unable to leave. She fled the only home she had without packing, and she had no friends in Houston and no family who would claim her.

I'd never met anyone like Linda. My face flushed red with shame at how insulated my privilege had left me and how powerless I felt to minister to someone my experience had not prepared me for. The more she shared, the more I realized how shaken we both were: me in my cluelessness and she in her spiritual, emotional, financial, and relational crisis. Her life was a raging and merciless storm. She had nothing and needed everything. I had no idea how to help.

What was God's good news for Linda here and now? What other tools did I need in my ministry toolkit besides the sinner's prayer? Her needs seemed overwhelming: emotional support, a safe place to sleep, a new job, confidential and free medical treatment, unconditional grace, a community that wouldn't flinch at her truth, evangelism, prayer, a mentor, a small group, a large group, an entirely new setting, freedom from shame, forgiveness of sin, forgiveness of debt, casseroles, new clothes, exorcism, assurance that God heard her cry, and love through human and divine hands. I could go on.

Was this a story about the brokenness of our world? Or was it a story about one young woman being lost? Was it about forces beyond her control or personal sinful decisions? As I prayed desperately to understand how to respond, God whispered in my ear, *Yes*. Yes, her world is broken, yes, her soul is starving, and yes, there is a solution: gospel.

In that moment I knew that God wept with her, and I knew, too, that Jesus weeps because our city doesn't know the things that make for peace. I knew that somehow and in some way, the gospel touches all life. Everything and everyone Linda needed to become fully human and abundantly alive God freely offers. God won't give up until the task is complete: "He will not grow faint or be crushed until he has established justice in the earth" (Isaiah 42:4).

Body, soul, mind, or city—which of these is healed by the gospel? Thankfully, we are not asked to choose. God is restoring all things—souls, streets, and entire cities—and invites us to be transformed with them.

FULLY HUMAN, FULLY ALIVE

But what exactly does that look and feel like in the real world? What does it mean to be truly mature? What are God's intentions for your life? For Christians, what is our image of full personhood? We are not the first to ask these questions! There are endless attempts at capturing what full personhood looks like. Barbie, Captain America, and Suburban Mom have each given it their best shot. Add to that anyone bent on embracing rugged individualism, keeping the world safe for democracy, keeping up with the Joneses, or continuing the steady climb toward the American dream. We buy "starter houses" and graduate to McMansions, right on schedule with our pay increase. We find refuge in being heterosexual, male, well educated, white: you name it. If it gives us a social boost or emotional pat on the back, we'll take it.

The ancient Greeks believed ideal personhood was about intellectual nobility. The Romans aspired to just power and the Hebrews to the righteousness of moral law. The classic image of mature personhood is Ulysses on a rugged and solitary quest, who returns home reborn with new and transformative knowledge.

Descartes said, "I think, therefore I am." Today we translate that as "I buy, therefore I am"; "I've arrived, therefore I am"; "I'm known . . ."; "I'm best . . ."; "I'm better than . . ." These are unconsciously the great goals in our human quest for life, liberty, and the pursuit of happiness.

Ours is a different story, though, and a fresh promise. We're exodus and resurrection people, called out of slavery to demons and wealth and selfishness into the freedom of new life in Christ. We're an odd folk, called to seek someone else's kingdom first and promised abundant life for doing so. We believe that breaking and pouring is the pattern that changes the world.

The early church worked hard to capture this in a meaningful way for their context, and they began to speak of Jesus as 100 percent human and 100 percent divine. Jesus was as human as I am in all my *in*capacity to live in radical submission to God, and as divine as the God whose mission is the restoration of all things.

This is good theology that pushes us to remember the Bible is a gritty book filled with blood and sweat and passions good and bad. In the midst of life lived in the here and now, Christ is revealed to be our model for life.

Imitating Christ is, for Paul, the key that frees us to find purpose. "The Son stands first in the line of humanity he restored. We see the original and intended shape of our lives there in him" (Romans 8:29 *The Message*).

Jesus—Son of Man and image of God—is the fullest and most transformative image of personhood the world has ever been offered. In his living and loving we see who we are meant to be: intimately connected to God, free to fully be ourselves, connected passionately to community, and committed to creating shalom in our world.

In the life of Jesus we find the world's first and finest workable life, a life of integrity and pure commitment to his guiding values, free of control from reputation, religiosity, and relatives. Without a doubt, Jesus is who I want to become when I grow up.

Former pope John Paul II said it in a speech full of spirit and invitation: "When you wonder about the mystery of yourself, look to Christ who gives you the meaning of life. When you wonder what it means to be a mature person, look to Christ who is the fullness of humanity. And when you wonder about your role in the future of the world, look to Christ."[1]

Jesus, not the Joneses, is how we see God's intent for all people. Jesus is the one foundation, and "no one can lay any foundation other than the one that has been laid" (1 Corinthians 3:11). Christ—the image of full humanity and life—captures the vision of a transformed life that gives itself away for the sake of the restoration of others to wholeness. His way of life stands in contrast to the consumer life, the religious life, the fearful life, and the self-centered life. That life is itself part of the gospel and part of the gift that frees us from lies that confuse our identity.

I say this because I have experienced this good news, and so have millions of others, and hopefully so have you. And I say this because it's the only way I can even begin to understand Linda's story, and my own. If I want to understand what *is*, I've got to catch a glimpse of what can be. Christ's life given for us and his lifestyle modeled for us are both gift and promise.

So if Jesus is the image of full personhood, what does that say about the people we live, work, and worship with? How does the gospel interpret and even diagnose the state of the human heart?

SPIRITUAL DETECTIVES

Realizing that Jesus was extraordinary at seeing people is a great place to start. There's just no other way of saying it. One look is all he needed to see straight into the human heart with transformative understanding, and straight through society with cutting insight. I may not have truly understood Linda and her potential, but Jesus has been with her since before birth. I've no doubt he knew intimately who she was.

---

1 Pope John Paul II, "To High School Students" (speech, Madison Square Garden, New York, October 3, 1979).

I recently spent an entire year reading detective mysteries to try to understand how Jesus did it. Odd places to look, perhaps, but consider the skills of detection required to size up individuals and uncover the story behind the story. Some of the most famous fictional detectives see individuals so accurately they're thought to be geniuses, if not psychics.

Sherlock Holmes was a master at seeing what others couldn't. "You know my method," he said. "It is founded upon the observation of trifles."[2] He could instantly discern intimate details with a glance at fingernails, mud stains, averted eyes, and heavy breathing. After one such uncanny and on-target assessment, his partner, Dr. Watson, said, "Like all Holmes's reasoning, the thing seemed simplicity itself when it was explained."[3]

While I don't hold out hope to be the next great intuitive detective, I do myself a disservice by dismissing Jesus' own intuition as nothing other than miraculous divine action.

Jesus is fully divine, absolutely. He is also fully human, with the gift of understanding people that freed him to love them precisely as they needed. "Jesus . . . knew all people and needed no one to testify about anyone; for he himself knew what was in everyone" (John 2:24-25). Jesus, the genius with insight and intuition, seems ready to take us on as apprentices in spiritual detection.

Equipped with the gospel, we too can be trained to see people through godly rather than human eyes. The early church certainly held out this hope. Paul says as much to the church at Corinth, "From now on, therefore, we regard no one from a human point of view; even though we once knew Christ from a human point of view, we know him no longer in that way" (2 Corinthians 5:16).

---

2 Sir Arthur Conan Doyle, "The Boscombe Valley Mystery," *The Complete Sherlock Holmes*, vol. 2 (New York: Doubleday, 1988), 214.
3 Sir Arthur Conan Doyle, "The Adventure of the Stockbroker's Clerk," *The Complete Sherlock Holmes*, vol. 2 (New York: Doubleday, 1988), 363.

Jesus knows we are created in the image of God, made a little lower than the angels and crowned with glory and honor. He knows too that we are filled with secret shame and uneasiness, beholden to unseen, unchosen forces we've inherited from the broken values of our age.

In Peter he sees both of these truths battling like hungry dogs. When Jesus first meets Peter he recognizes him to be a rock, and yet later unmasks his hidden fears as having near demonic power.

Jesus takes one look at Nathaniel and knows instantly he is "an Israelite in whom there is no deceit" (John 1:47). And it only gets better from here.

He knows how to turn a woman's sordid past into an authentic gospel invitation for neighbors (John 4).

He knows the busiest among us may have the most to run from.

He knows that the rich need to make reparations and the poor need debts forgiven.

He knows our insatiable need to feel better than others and tells stories that unmask it (the eldest prodigal son, laborers in the vineyard, the Pharisees trying to stone a woman).

He knows that poverty can lead to rich faith and riches to a poverty of faith.

He knows when to accuse and when to forgive, when to throw tables and when to eat at them.

He knows when to point out existing conflict and when to save people from it.

He knows about the destructive power of lust and our lust for destruction.

He knows we want privilege and need downward mobility. He knows our passion to preserve life and our need to lose it.

He knows who is blind and who can see, and he knows when that has nothing to do with physical sight.

Jesus sees how the crowds are blinded by messianic expectations of David's empire come again, and weeps that such a mistake could lead to destruction—which it did.

Over and over again, the Gospels tell the story of an intuitive man who sees people as they truly are, and in doing so brings them hope.

Jesus was and remains a genius detective of the human predicament.

Jesus doesn't look at mere trifles, observing tiny details to diagnose the needs of those he meets; nor is he a psychic. He looks at individuals—he looks at *us*—through the eyes of the gospel. His measure of a woman isn't religion, reputation, class, or education. It is gospel: the fullness of God offered to the full ness of humanity.

This is local, boots-on-the-ground customized intelligence; table by table, door by door, heart by human heart. It is not universal law, common sense, or systematic theology. It is walk-outside-your-door, down-past-the-office-cubicles, shake-the-hand-of-the-woman-next-to-you love of neighbor. It contains the capacity to change the world.

As a survivor of childhood sexual abuse—complete with all the shame and defensive routines that come with survival—I'm not always certain I want people to look at me this personally—or, frankly, to see me at all. Every so often I'm reminded of how traumatic it was for me as a teenager to simply walk in front of a gymnasium or lunchroom crowd. Reading the Gospels can feel a bit like that, or like walking through a security scanner at the airport: there's nothing I can hide! But this is a gift of God's Word, which is "able to judge the thoughts and intentions of the heart" (Hebrews 4:12).

I had this same feeling when I was with Linda—that being *seen* simply terrified her. At the same time, being seen was the greatest gift, and one that she needed so desperately. She needed someone to see and understand, to see and accept, to see and speak the truth in love.

I've had to learn again and again that being seen by Jesus is *good* news and nothing to fear. Jesus' exposé brings new life and healing—the stunning feeling of being accepted despite all the condemnation and shame we've allowed to fester. It took a while for Linda, but being seen, with grace and respect, eventually became good news for her. And nothing—not water or war, worry or want—is outside Jesus' perception. He knows you and loves you exactly as you are.

We have been created to dance, and yet we find our hearts unable to do what we long to do and our feet tripped up by forces outside our control. The freedom found in Christ liberates both our hearts and feet to move to the music of God unhindered. Jesus has come to set us free on the inside and out.

A TOUR OF WIDENING LOVE

I wish it were as easy as that sounds! Actually, Paul is clear in other letters that we can't choose our way to seeing people from God's perspective. He prays in the first chapter of Ephesians that we'd have eye-opening faith to see the fullness of what is promised. If we want to get mission right, we simply have to get Jesus right.

In the weeks after meeting Linda, I knew I needed more eye-opening faith. Soon I found myself on a bus filled with low-wage workers whose employers had stolen from them, touring Houston and hearing their stories. We called it the "justice bus," because as a group of employees and their allies, we were visiting workplaces and meeting with employers who were treating workers unjustly.

Along the way, from one business to the next (one business was even in my own neighborhood), I heard these employees' stories. They ceased being strangers and became people with families and hopes. Seeing the city through their eyes clarified lines of poverty and wealth, fear and safety, and taught me, as Linda had, how wide and deep God's concern is for all people.

Jesus' extraordinary ability to see leads naturally to an equally intense compassion. With the eyes of our hearts enlightened, compassion can become our default as well, our primary way of seeing people right off the bat. Care as lived by Jesus and taught in the New Testament is the beating heart of Christian ethics. Love is the more excellent way to live, precisely because God is love. This truth is beautiful enough to heal our hearts so we can be healers of community.

The foundation of such a loving life is embracing God's love for us, regardless: God is restoring us to wholeness. Just as Jesus before us, we are recipients of God's limitless love.

Since that tour, I've taken and led other tours of specific neighborhoods to dig through the layers of time to understand the stories and injustices they hold. I'll never forget how transformative a two-hour bus tour of known human trafficking sites was for me. Learning for the first time how present this evil is, I instantly began to see victims, their employers, and myself differently. Even more important was to witness how God was using the ministry to bring freedom and hope. How could I be silent in the face of such injustice? How could my definition of Christianity insulate me any longer from God's work to stop injustice?

Like Jesus, who taught his disciples by pointing out things along the way, churches and faith-based nonprofits are increasingly using neighborhood tours to help Christians understand where they live. Tours can help us see current reality and live faithfully.

This was definitely true of a man named Chopper, who, on a bus tour of the Spring Branch neighborhood of Houston, learned to see his migrant neighbors with new eyes. A life-long resident of one of Houston's oldest black neighborhoods, Chopper is no stranger to how race works in America. But having heard the stories of five migrants without documents, dangerous stories about coyote smugglers, and inspiring stories of faith, Chopper turned to his tour guide and said, "I got to talk to you."

Chopper had always thought immigrants were in the country illegally to steal his job. But eating with these Christian men, he now knew differently. "They're just feeding their families like everyone else," he said. "They're brothers and sisters in Christ more connected to me than a thousand unsaved neighbors."

Chopper's learning to see these fellow Christians with new eyes would alone make for a beautiful story. But Chopper also began to see *himself* with new eyes. Later, in a moment of courageous authenticity, he said to the group, "I think I'm a racist." This is not an easy thing for any of us to say out loud, and saying it blanketed the room with anxiety. Most of us just aren't used to this level of honesty. It would have been easy to dismiss his admission, bringing the discomfort in the room back down to a welcome level. But Chopper and his team pressed in rather than pulling back, and found in the tension the hope of liberation from an ancient lie that bound them all. For everyone who shared Chopper's experience and conversation that hot summer day, new possibilities of faithfulness flourished.

The gospel begins to wean us from our need to earn love through appearances or expectations, through white supremacist standards or black-on-brown competition. We are the beloved of God, who calls us to love as we have ourselves been loved. Taking tours and learning stories and meeting people face-to-face are fundamental ways we can break down stereotypes and see people as people, not projects. Seeing is becoming, so to speak, and helps us default to love in our choices and mission.

FREEDOM FOR OTHERS

This brings me back to my story with Linda, and to Jesus, who I've already said was extraordinary at seeing people. The only way I could make sense of Linda's predicament was by trying to see her as God does. It's the only way my heart could find the compassion to love her as she needs.

But Linda's unexpected presence on my church's front porch was also a story about me. And my story—no less than Linda's—needs to be understood through the lens of the gospel.

She stirred up a host of emotions in me, and they all pointed to one highly guarded secret in my life: I want you to like me. I *need* you to like me; it's the only way I know how to feel good about myself. Performance is my habit, and it's worked well for years.

Ever since childhood, my identity has been wrapped up in being good. Kids get their strokes in all kinds of ways—athletics, grades, being the clown—but for me it was morals. It's a simple formula, really: do good + be good + be seen as good = feel good.

When I first invited God into my heart, it was a faulty God, an incomplete God—an elf-on-the-shelf God who nitpicked every detail of sin and demanded confession. Overwhelming pangs of guilt were always welcome. Mine was a God who asked a lot and gave little. I learned to come to God the way I came to church: clean and tidy, with shirt tucked in and nails properly clipped. I felt little choice in learning to hide significant portions of my true self from God and the people who loved me.

I didn't get it. I didn't understand that there's no such thing as a scarcity of love, in which God divvies up resources to the deserving. And so I worked tirelessly to earn what I could not feel had already been given. And it was an impossible, exhausting endeavor—trying to "want" myself to faithfulness without drinking deeply from the presence of the risen Christ.

Here's why this matters, and why it's essential for my ministry that I root around in the unevangelized places of my past and cut off their inertia. My addiction to approval meant I wasn't wired to see people as people; I was wired to see people as opportunities. People like Linda were objects: problems I could solve and a potential ministry success that might earn your respect. I can't truly love you, or see you as Jesus does, if the storm raging in my soul screams for you to approve of me.

I became fairly adept at quieting the voice within that whispered I wasn't good enough. Indeed, I can self-soothe with the best of us. I remember pointed moments as a child when my obedience was rewarded by adults broadcasting my goodness to other adults. Yep, that's right: I built my self-image on secondhand approval. And all because I have believed a lie: a lie that says I am not good enough, that my self-worth comes from others. It's a tragic tale that has consumed incredible energy to protect my wounded self. That little shame voice has spoken up numerous times even as I write this book, telling me I'm doing this just so you'll like me (and if not you, maybe the kid who beat me up in middle school).

It's a patterned spiritual poverty that leads many of us to habitual unfaithfulness: I'm not good enough, and so I'll do what I need to earn self-worth. I'm addicted to approval, and I'll get it as a do-gooder. I need God to see me as good, and I'll do what's needed to prove I am.

I wonder what emotions this stirs up in you. I wonder if you can see how very much more God wants for me, and for Linda. Can you sense God's mind-boggling aspirations for human flourishing, and how far we fall short? Do you see something in your own life—some anxiety or hidden fear—that blocks you from loving others?

Seeing myself as God does stirs in me a powerful hunger for the abundant life that Jesus promised, a life of liberation from the expectations *from* others so I'm free to live *for* others. This isn't so much a life I can will myself into as it is a life I'm freed to live. It's a life I'm given as a natural response to who and how God is.

Paul said it beautifully, "I *have found the freedom to* truly live for God. I have been crucified with the Anointed One—I am no longer alive—but the Anointed is living in me" (Galatians 2:19-20 The Voice). Owning my story makes me hungry not merely for a personal relationship with God but for an intimate one.

Here is the heart of the heart of the heart of our capacity to love: "by grace you have been saved" (Ephesians 2:8). Grace is the hinge between the inner life of faith and the outer life of love. God isn't watching from some distant shelf to see if we do what's demanded. God is showering us with grace as spiritual empowerment for the life Jesus modeled for us to live.

Our value and worth do not come by being better, different, greater, smarter, stronger, faster, richer, or more beautiful. We do not gain personal value through social acceptance or salvation through competition. Nor can we ever alone overcome the sense that we're just not good enough. Our place in community, our belovedness despite our faults, our self-identity, and our ability to love others come by allowing ourselves to be defined by God and God alone.

Wanting transformation and living it are two very different things. For Linda, seeing in Christ the beauty of a life fully human and fully alive was a stronger inspiration to change her life than hitting rock bottom had been. There was more to life and far greater promises than the painful life she previously thought she deserved. Her path to healing has been a journey of thousands of small decisions. She has needed countless reminders of God's love, infinite patience from communities who have accepted her as she is, and the hard truth spoken about the gaps she's still living in. She has learned—and taught me—this: transformation is both a choice and a gift. We can't in and of ourselves change; but we can be changed.

Linda is enough. You are enough. I am enough. I am saved by grace with nothing to prove. I am created a little lower than the angels and crowned with glory and honor. And I'm in relationship with a God who sees me as I am, and rejoices over me with singing.

Who doesn't want more of that?

FIVE

Evangelizing Peace

THE SANTOS and Esther Nieto Park in Houston is like most of the parks I've taken my children to in the city. Kids swing and run around in blissful unawareness; youth play basketball and swap news; parents sit on benches, thankful for a moment of respite. But in the middle of this glorious swirl of urban relationships is a startling mural that offers a kind of contextual theology of the sort we're after here.

A mournful mother sits and holds her dying son, limp across her lap. He's depicted as a local boy, perhaps a Latino gang member, wearing the clothes and colors of this neighborhood. He's been wounded mortally by our transgressions. The mother and child appear to be in the streets, on a stoop right outside their door, miles and moments too far from any hospital to matter. His life was taken from him right where he lived it.

Artistically the mother resembles Jesus' mother, Mary: her eyes helpless in the face of death, her head crowned and haloed in the classic pietà fashion. Somehow, in the shock of the moment, she has pulled her son's heavy body onto her lap, cradling him as only a parent could. Perhaps in this neighborhood he was their hope for salvation and a future. And here he lies dying.

I can imagine his mother scolding him repeatedly for his dangerous lifestyle, words ultimately helpless to stop terror, trauma, and violence. And so she grieves, and does the only thing she can in the moment: she cares for the dying.

It strikes me how often this scene has been repeated in the streets of Houston: dying sons and weeping mothers caught in a culture of poverty, beholden to the myth that violence will bring redemption and devastated by its utter failure to bring change. We live in a culture that too often values destroying life and not helping it to flourish.

Is this mural how the neighborhood perceives the church? Are we like Mary in this mural—offering too little too late, irrelevant in the face of violence, tending the wounds of our sons but incapable of preventing them? Is it possible we've resigned ourselves to the role of postchaos chaplain and missed opportunities to stop violence before it erupts?

On the surface, the Christian story addresses violence almost as much as any topic. The main character in our story escaped countless violent attempts on his life, stopped leaders from killing women, condemned his followers for suggesting a Hiroshima-like destruction of cities, and healed a man's cut-off ear. He taught us that if you live by violence, you can expect to die by violence. He taught us that "an eye for an eye" is completely antithetical to a God-faithful life. Perhaps Jesus' story has more to say about violence than we've thought. The ancient prophets promised a Messiah was coming who would bring salvation from violence and create a new, peaceable, enemy-less community of faith. I don't think we can understand Jesus without understanding this chosen prophetic stream; nor can we understand the prophet's promise of shalom without witnessing its fulfillment in Jesus. It's a bit of a chicken-and-egg scenario. We'll look in this chapter at how Jesus lived out God's gift of peace, and in the next section explore the ancient path of shalom, so essential to understanding who and how God is in our world.

JESUS' PEACE SIGN

Locked in my memory is a trip my five-year-old son and I took to a friend's house for breakfast. A few days before, my son had asked me if it was mean for David to kill Goliath. Their story is featured prominently on the cover of my son's copy of *The Beginner's Bible*, and so of course it was a favorite. The picture depicts a jubilant and victorious David, laughing and praising God. My son had been understandably confused; why did David get to celebrate killing someone when he was punished for being mean? I had told him I thought he was right, and that sometimes the Bible tells stories to teach us what *not* to do. And I mentioned how later God told David he'd been too violent to build God's house. My son had assured me if he was ever mad at someone, he wouldn't hit them with rocks or swords.

On a cool fall morning a few days later, my son's theological wheels were spinning. Spotting a cross on the side of the road, he shouted, "Look, Dad, a peace sign!" This may be the very pinnacle of his theological career, and if so, he's in great company.

Paul basically said the same thing in Colossians when he wrote that "God was pleased to reconcile to himself all things, whether on earth or in heaven, by making peace through the blood of his cross" (Colossians 1:20). The definitive moment in salvation history, in which God makes peace with humanity, is the exact moment in which humanity declares war on God. Like a rainbow painted across the sky, Jesus' cross speaks the message of God's peace with all creation.

I've always been fascinated by how you get from the story of a thing to theology. How exactly did the early church get from the crime scene of Jesus' cross to the theology that says somehow his murder created peace in our world?

If ever there was a case where forgiveness is absolutely uncalled for, it was the injustice of God's own Son being killed. When humanity butchers God, you don't just expect retribution; you have earned the right of a Noah 2.0 absolute punishment, or a Gomorrah revisited. In the time of Noah, God was saddened with humanity's violence so deeply that, so says the story, God hit the reset button on the whole project.

And yet, at the precise moment one would expect divine anger to boil over into tit for tat, Jesus refuses every form of retribution imaginable. Instead of a justifiable war cry, all we hear from Jesus is a countersentence: "Father, forgive them; for they do not know what they are doing" (Luke 23:34). He stops hate in its tracks and offers an utterly surprising gift in return: "Peace be with you" (John 20:19, 21).

Lethal force is abandoned; all we hear from Jesus is that we are not Public Enemy No. 1. God says you are forgiven for killing God.

When Jesus is dead and hidden away in a locked tomb, it looks to be the perfect crime—except for one small aspect of the story. He doesn't stay dead.

Over and over again, the New Testament uses the death and resurrection of Jesus to point us to the good news that it is this peaceable God who is Lord of all. It's an equation outlined simply as: Jesus' death + Jesus' resurrection = Jesus is glorified by God as Lord of all.[1]

Saying that Jesus' resurrection makes him God and King is clearly a theological statement about the divinity of Christ. But equally so, and perhaps just as important for North American Christians to ponder, is its clarity about the Jesus-likeness of God. On a cross high on a Judean hill, God is revealed to be like Jesus.

The gospel is not about me; it's about what God is doing in human history and how God chooses to do it. God knows that we're caught up in the injustices around us, that family and social experiences entangle us, and that unevangelized zones of our past bind us. And so God is a God of liberation, personal transformation, and new hope. God knows that our world is caught in a suicidal spin cycle of violence, and God has chosen the incarnation of Jesus Christ to address our affliction.

Thankfully, we don't get to choose what God is up to. What we do find is the ministry of God's Messiah deeply tied up with overcoming violence, which tells me that violence is at the core of human brokenness. Can we be fully human and fully alive while still bound by the assumption of violence? Can we become children of God without making peace and doing it in the way that Jesus did?

No, this is not a story about me. This is a story about God and the redemption of all things—things on earth and things in heaven. It's the story of a man named Jesus who stopped violence in its tracks—killing *killing*, so to speak—and left us free for human community at a level we never would have dared imagine possible. It's at Jesus' peace sign—a Roman cross of

---

1 You can see this gospel formula in Peter (Acts 2:22-36); Paul (Romans 1:4; 1 Corinthians 15:24-28; Ephesians 1:19-23; Philippians 2:8-9; Colossians 1:18; 2:15); John (John 17:5; Revelation 4–5); and Hebrews (10:12-13).

execution—where we most clearly understand what God is doing in human history and how God chose to do it.

God does not need to destroy in order to make peace. God
does not need to punish before he loves. God does not need to
be wrathful before forgiving. God does not need to kill the one
in order to save the many. The gospel, as it turns out, is the God
of peace!

Maybe this shouldn't surprise us. After all, Jesus merely took
the ancient prophets at their word and lived as though their
promises were true. It's okay to burn our uniforms, repurpose
our weapons, and refuse standing armies—not as a moral im-
perative but because we trust in the Lord our God and believe
the good news of Jesus above all else. Jesus trusted God's sovereignty and became a living testimony to the possibility of
nonviolence.

In a time as complex and dangerous as our own, Jesus lived
as if the long-awaited kingdom were actually already here. The
prophets envisioned a time when learning the skills of war
would be obsolete, and so Jesus lived as though those skills
were already useless. Jesus read in his Scripture that we'll have
no enemies in the new age, and so Jesus refused to have any in
his age. Jesus lived as if God's kingdom and will were truly present on earth as they are in heaven—and that included the path
of nonviolence.

For those of us who still think that God is active in our world,
this is, according to Jesus, what God is doing. Jesus claimed to
do nothing but mimic what he saw God doing (John 5:19-20).

In his teachings and living, Jesus repeatedly addressed violence head-on, bringing us freedom from its harm in our streets
and its hate in our hearts. Like slaves spirited to freedom on the
Underground Railroad, Jesus' gospel frees us from chains and
cultures of violence. Paul prays in Colossians 1:13 that we've

been rescued from their grasp and not left to our own devices, and that we find our safety in God's promised kingdom of peace.

It's no wonder Paul felt he needed to say he wasn't ashamed of the gospel. Its message is completely downside up from what we might expect. And yet it's this gospel message that makes things right in the world. Evil has been defeated, and death is no more. The resurrection of the executed Jesus is the final word in God's affirmation that the way of Christ is the best way to live.

In the best news the world has ever heard, God turns out to be just like Jesus.

A REMARKABLE ADVERTISEMENT FOR GOD

My friend David Atwood lives that truth as if it's the air he breathes. He long ago began to take Jesus at his word and accept Jesus' story as good news for the world we live in.

When David and his wife, Peggy, first moved to Houston in the 1970s, he was an oil executive for the Shell Oil Company. Soon after arriving, they moved again into an impoverished neighborhood and slowly got involved in spiritual activities focused on the poor. After a ten-year period of what he calls "personal development and transformation," David had grown increasingly interested in what was happening to those around him.

The more he saw and heard, the more his heart was filled with compassion for the kind of folks he saw Jesus caring for in Scripture. It wouldn't be a stretch to say that meeting Houston's most vulnerable members was like a second conversion for David. It was here that he truly grew to believe Jesus.

This newfound belief and the compassion that accompanied it led him to a most unexpected place. Death row was not then nor now a typical place to spend your free time. But it is where we house the worst of the worst among us—those we easily assume to be our enemies—and David could not escape the simplicity of Jesus' invitation to love enemies.

It was as simple yet counterintuitive as that: Do we or don't we believe Jesus when he says those words? Do we believe Jesus when he says we become children of God by making peace, not revenge? Do we take him at his word that visiting prisoners is like a face-to-face visit with Christ? Over time David grew to understand that if you want to make peace, you've got to go where there is conflict.

And so to Texas' death row he went, and went, and went— hundreds of times. Visiting inmates, murderers, and men wracked with guilt and affliction, he met the worst of the worst, and he learned to love. David talks about how meeting these convicted men and their families helped him to see them as human beings. No matter what they've done, his faith taught him to lead with compassion and to treat them as equals.

David has told me before that Jesus' command to love our enemies is the hardest thing that's ever been said. And yet he has testified, "I can say I love some people on death row that I visited for a long time." David's growing belief and growing love has led him to be one of Texas' strongest supporters of abolishing the death penalty. For him, his behavior isn't about morals or politics, though he is excellently skilled in both types of arguments. For him, it is all about God's kingdom in the here and now.

David has spent as much time inside death row as he has at vigils outside the nation's busiest execution chamber. He has sat with family members through too many executions to count, and with legislators through too many meetings to remember. His work has helped overturn multiple convictions and set men free for crimes they were unjustly imprisoned for.

David was present to see Dominique Green die by lethal injection at 7:59 p.m. on October 26, 2004. David commented later about how at peace Dominique's soul was, even when his world was crashing down. No matter how horribly he was treated or how innocent he believed himself to be, Dominique was never bitter. Instead he chose to embrace his unique location as a place of mission. While living on death row for a crime he didn't commit, Dominique led many of his fellow Texas death row inmates to forgive everyone who had hurt them and to seek forgiveness from anyone they had harmed.

When Archbishop Desmond Tutu met Dominique Green behind bars, he said it was like being "in the presence of God" and called him "a remarkable advertisement for God."[2] Dominique's neighborhood might not have looked anything like mine, but he most certainly lived a life of radical faith right where he was!

David Atwood's ministry to those in prison isn't limited to the feel-good stories of converted inmates. Neither guilt nor innocence, monstrous truth nor faulty defense, separates David from his sense of call to mirror God's limitless love. "The real key to bringing forth the kingdom of God on this planet," he said in a sermon he preached during my church's worship, "is that we go and meet with the people we deem to be the enemy."

David's dogged trust in Jesus' way of addressing violence blurs the lines between personal ministry and social justice. His love for our enemies reminds me that the alternative lifestyle of Jesus is a remarkable advertisement for God.

WHOSE PEACE IS GOSPEL: CAESAR'S OR CHRIST'S?

If I had told you the story of Dominique Green without mention that his ministry was on death row, his story would hardly be worth telling. The same is true of David Atwood—if all I

---

2 Michael Graczyk, "Desmond Tutu Visits Texas Death Row Inmate," *My Plain View*, March 24, 2004, http://www.myplainview.com/article_49f5495b -25e9-5679-a721-8936900dbebf.html.

mentioned was his love for everyone, but didn't tell you he loves men on death row, his story would also be unremarkable. Their stories become powerful when we know who they have chosen to love and where those people live.

I can't imagine a story where the context is more important than the story of Jesus. His story would be hard to understand if we didn't know that his death came about as a state-sponsored, religiously motivated public execution.

Everything about Jesus and his theology, everything about the way that the New Testament talks about Jesus, was all in this unique context. Jesus, Paul, and John all borrow explicitly political, explicitly Roman vocabulary to make sense of Jesus' mission in the world. Words like *gospel*, *kingdom*, *Son of God*, *peace*, *Lord*, and even *salvation* are borrowed directly from Roman political culture.

This doesn't appear to be accidental. The political ruler of the day used the exact same words to describe himself. Out of all the words Jesus could have used to describe his own message, he used the word *gospel*, which means good news from the front lines of battle, to talk about his way in the world. The New Testament contrasts the story of the Roman Empire with Jesus' kingdom, begging the question, is Jesus or Caesar Lord? Is the news about Jesus or Caesar good news? Whose gospel can actually bring peace?

This is not a "You say po-ta-to, I say po-tah-to" kind of thing. This is a red-pill, rabbit-hole, walk-through-the-wardrobe, two-roads-diverged type of choice. Our answer to the question matters, exceptionally. "Enter through the narrow gate; for the gate is wide and the road is easy that leads to destruction, and there are many who take it" (Matthew 7:13).

Brian Zahnd tells his story of conversion to Jesus' gospel of peace in his amazing book *A Farewell to Mars*. "What happened was once the red, white, and blue varnish was removed from Jesus and I learned to read the Gospels free of a star-spangled interpretation, I discovered that my Lord and Savior had a lot of things to say about peace that I had been missing."[3]

To make sense of Jesus' story, we need to understand that every act of violence is performed with a good reason in mind. In other words, Rome's cross was also a peace sign.

Torture and terror were how Caesar tried to keep the peace in his realm. He actually believed that killing would sustain the status quo.[4] And Jesus, who came announcing the presence of a new kingdom under the nose of Caesar, was turning this assumption upside down. Rome called this method of pacification "Peace and safety" and "Peace through victory." It wasn't that they intentionally killed the Son of God; they genuinely believed violence created the common good.

Caesar isn't alone in operating this way. For thousands of years, governments have attempted to make peace through violence. Aristotle said, "We make war that we may live in peace." George Washington mirrored these sentiments: "To be prepared for war is one of the most effective means of preserving peace." Modern governments still function in this same way, believing preventive war can and will bring peace.

And it's not just in politics, either. John allows us to sit in on a closed-door meeting in which the religious elites chose administrative violence as the solution to the Jesus problem: "It is better for you to have one man die for the people than to have the whole nation destroyed" (John 11:50). For Caiaphas, killing Jesus was a way of keeping peace for his people.

What was Jesus doing that created enough fear in the leaders that they simply had to make a spectacle of him? To put the

---

3 Zahnd, *A Farewell to Mars*, 136.
4 The early church had thoughts on the slogan "Peace and security", see 1 Thessalonians 5:3.

question bluntly: Why in the world did the good news Jesus lived and proclaimed get him killed?

Perhaps it was precisely because he was announcing the presence of a new *kingdom* and a new way to make *peace*. He was, as we have already seen, announcing the good news, directed primarily to the most vulnerable. The good news was that Jesus' alternative ideas about politics and peace were true and possible to live today. This message, which thrilled some, terrified those in power.

Reading the gospel stories reveals that the culture in which we find ourselves also holds values that destroy life rather than empower it to thrive. We are left, again and again, with the question of whose peace we believe is good news and whose gospel actually makes peace. Christian theology is unrelenting on this point. Jesus' cross unmasks the "peacemaking" ways of Caesar as behaviorally bankrupt. You cannot live the gospel of Caesar while worshiping the God of Jesus' gospel. You cannot put people on a cross (or execution table or tree) and understand the true meaning of Jesus' cross.

Killing gang members, as the Nieto Park mural depicts, is not a neighborhood improvement plan. Neither guns on our streets nor nukes in hidden silos can bring us the life-giving peace that Jesus' way of life reveals. Regardless of what Hollywood and religious groups may say, violence will never bring our communities redemption.

KILLING *KILLING*

Caesar's way of bringing good into our world is simply not up to the job of making peace. Paul says in Colossians 2:15 that Jesus' cross is a huge exposé, for it is here Jesus "disarmed the rulers and authorities and made a public example of them, triumphing over them in it."

Paul is even more colorful in his letter to the Ephesus church, writing in Ephesians that Jesus "kill[s] off" hostility (Ephesians 2:16 The Voice). The work of the cross is the killing of killing. Jesus isn't fighting people but the spiritual realities of hostility, hatred, and exclusion. Every false narrative, every violent means to the good, every psychologically sick reality that divides and excludes humanity, Jesus is putting to death.

In place of our need for enemies, Jesus creates "one new humanity in place of the two, thus making peace. . . . You are no longer strangers and aliens, but you are citizens with the saints and also members of the household of God" (Ephesians 2:15, 19).

More than any other law, code, philosophy, or worldview in history, the Roman cross upon which Jesus was executed shows us the world as it truly is and as God intends for it to be. If you want to understand the brokenness of the world, look to the sins that nailed Jesus to the cross. If you want to see God's response to violence, look to the love that held Jesus on the cross. If you want to understand evil in the world, look to the good that people tried to accomplish by executing Jesus. If you want to know what God is doing in our world, look to the peaceable forgiveness offered to friends and enemies alike by the resurrected one among us.

This has been the personal journey of Air Force officer Glen Guyton. He started his adult life in a socially accepted path to the American dream, at the Air Force Academy in Colorado Springs. With Christ in his heart, he was ready to live the life he wanted and his culture affirmed. At the time, he felt no dissonance between his faith and his military service. But slowly Christ began to show him "a still more excellent way" (1 Corinthians 12:31).

Glen's invitation to Jesus was infinitely expanded when he accepted Jesus' invitation to him—"Come, follow me." Christ's was a subversive and radical love—a fiercely loyal love of God, honest love of self, committed love of neighbor, and transforming love of enemy. Believing in Jesus led him to believe Jesus. Love of enemy not only was possible; it was more efficient in bringing the good all of us seek.

The more clearly Glen saw Jesus' way of peace, the more he felt called to give his allegiance to no one else. For him, living in the gospel required a surgical separation of faith from the American glorification of power, wealth, and violence. He came to see he simply could not grow as a Jesus-follower while aligned so firmly with the very powers from which we need to be saved. Glen came to understand that Jesus' way of making peace is not through the killing of others, but through the killing of killing. The only way to "defeat" an enemy is to stop having enemies altogether.

A SPONGE FOR HATE

This was a message so freeing that when the early church authors were looking for a summary of Jesus' life, they said, in a kind of tweetable summary, that Jesus was evangelizing people with the gift of peace.

Jesus' action in Ephesians 2:17 has been translated in a variety of ways, including that he "preached peace" and "proclaimed peace."[5] But a direct quote of the Greek in Ephesians 2:17 would read that Jesus "evangelized peace." The Voice translation says, "The Great Preacher of Peace . . . came for you." I think that was the author's creative way of saying that peace is the essence of gospel, as impossible to separate as it would be to unscramble eggs. This is the message and new reality that shines in the darkness of our death-dealing world.

---

5 "Preached peace" appears in, among others, the NIV, NET, NCV, and KJV translations; "proclaimed peace" appears in the NRSV.

Jesus is most assuredly not letting evil have its way in spreading the word about peace. He is not being passive or advocating a flight mentality. He is offering a third way between fight and flight, a way that addresses violence head-on by absorbing its hate. Peter says that "when [Christ] was abused, he did not return abuse; when he suffered, he did not threaten; but he entrusted himself to the one who judges justly" (1 Peter 2:23). Jesus' creative response stops violence in its tracks.

Jesus teaches us to return evil with goodness precisely because he understands evil more than anyone else in the history of humanity. Like Caesar's war gospel, Jesus' peace gospel also comes complete with a lifestyle of faithfulness in daily life. There's a script for this, a set of skills, a way of being in the world for everyday Christian peacemakers. Believing Jesus (not merely believing *in* Jesus) frees us to accept God's invitation to become children of God by making peace.

Remarkably, this is not only an action; it's also a promise. Before the cross, Jesus invites us to see ourselves as followers; after the cross, he promises us the power of the executed and now-risen Christ within us. Peace as the gift of God comes as the Christ-breathed gift of Spirit.

This is a gospel lifestyle! It's not extra credit, or an elective, or a special track of special action for special people, the privileged few. This is the kind of life we'd naturally live if we truly believed Jesus' gospel. It is action rooted in theology, behavior rooted in belief, and discipleship rooted in the story of Jesus.

Reconciliation is the heart of the gospel we're invited to share with our world. Drawing on Isaiah's imaginative vision of the peaceable kingdom, Jesus calls his followers to be makers of peace rather than judgment and discord, and he gives us specific instructions on how to pull it off.

In other words, Jesus asks us to be radically free. Free from retribution, free from reciprocity, free from emotional bursts of hate and anger, free from bitterness, free from defensiveness and the need for vengeance. Free for radical self-identity. Free to find our identity in God alone. Free to treat people based on our character and not theirs. Free to love as we've been loved by God, not treated by enemies. Free to believe the gospel of Jesus Christ.

PEACE CAMP

As a father of three and a pastor to families, it's this freedom I hope to share with my three little peacemakers. But how can we become more like Jesus, who naturally absorbed violence and lived in enemy-less community?

My wife and I pass on our faith to our kids by sharing our love for God and all things Jesus. We talk and sing a lot about Jesus' love for our kids and for all people. We talk a lot about God's creativity in making so many cool things (birds, bees, and trees; all the colors of the rainbow; amazing and different cultures) and how thankful we are that God created our little ones just the way they are.

We try hard to instill the both/and of God's love: that God loves them deeply and completely, and that God loves everyone they'll ever meet deeply and completely. And so when we recite the Lord's Prayer, I make it clear this is a prayer to *our* Father and for a huge *us*, which includes everyone and not just our family.

We cannot ask our kids to *do* something different without teaching them a different way to *be*. This, in a nutshell, is the vision of Houston's Peace Camp, a creative alternative summer day camp for children and youth that trains everyday peacemakers.

Hosted by our church, Peace Camp embraces the wild truth that children's ministry is an utterly subversive and hope-filled act. At Peace Camp we learn to see ourselves as "us" rather than "us and them."

Peace Camp lives that out by welcoming all kids regardless of their religion or ability to pay. When I walk into our sanctuary during Peace Camp, I see my kids learning alongside Muslim kids, gay kids, nonreligious kids, Jewish kids. It looks like Houston, a tiny microcosm of reality and the promise of God's multicultural banquet in heaven. Kids are taught radical acceptance and creative cooperation through both the curriculum and their method of being together.

Just to clarify: Peace Camp is forming peacemakers, not peacekeepers. Peace*keepers* are people-pleasers who just want everyone to get along. Peacekeepers try to be really nice, and are often very quiet, but in doing so they may enable divisive behavior to remain unchallenged. On the other hand, peace*makers* work to create conditions for peace, no matter the cost.

So Peace Camp helps children, in age-appropriate ways, to analyze social forms of discrimination, narratives of "us versus them," and the lies of superiority. It's a curriculum to empower youth with the skills to repair broken relationships. Youth learn how to understand and deal with difficult people and bullies. Younger kids learn how to say no, and older youth learn the skills of being an ally and defending the defenseless.

One participant said, "I learned that it is okay to get angry, but not to hurt anyone."

It's easy for churches with traditional youth programs to miss a truth Jesus dares us to imagine: that youth aren't just recipients of ministry; they are called to participate in the here and now. The abundant life of wholeness and health that Jesus promised is the life of radical faithfulness, and that's as true for youth as it is for teachers and boardroom executives. Youth ministry isn't about saving kids but about helping them find their place in God's story.

And so we teach our children the skills of active peacemaking and bringing transformation to our city. We do this for the simple reason that Jesus is making peace in Houston and has asked us to join him.

When I put my three children to bed, I always bless them. The handful of times in the last two years I've forgotten, my son exclaims, "Dad, you didn't bless me!" He smiles literally every time I say the words: "Grace to you and peace. May you always know you are loved, may you always love God, always love yourself, and love everyone that God loves—which is everybody you'll ever meet."

SIX

Form a New Disciple-Making Culture

ON THE SPRING DAY in 2010 when I published my first *Peace Pastor* blog post for the *Houston Chronicle*, I shook with fear—literally. I had written similar articles numerous times, but this was different. This was public—really public, and on a huge platform.

When the newspaper first asked me to write for them as a religious leader, they wooed me, complimented me, and zeroed in on how distinct it was to have a pastor in Houston talking about peace and Jesus in the same sentence. Later I asked a friend if I should accept their invitation, and he told me straight up, "The world doesn't need more people talking about peace. We need more people talking about Jesus as the source of peace in our world. Without Jesus, it's just babbling words."

And so I began to write about Jesus; Jesus and Houston, Jesus and the death penalty, Jesus and schools and hunger and racism and war and peace. Jesus present and passionate about the people I know and the neighborhoods they live in.

But what I wrote that first year isn't what sticks in my mind. What I remember is how I felt. I still can feel my sweaty hands and how alone it felt to have my neck stuck out further than I assumed my church wanted it to be. My fear wasn't only coming from the blogging but from all the fears about ministry I'd had in the past. Several years before this I'd been asked to leave a ministry position, and the shame of that failure had nearly overwhelmed me. It left me afraid of rocking the boat or upsetting someone in my congregation so much that they'd stop coming or ask me to do the same. I made a decision at that time that I would never ruffle feathers in my ministry or jeopardize my reputation again. I would play it safe at all costs. So when I hit the Publish button, my anxiety wasn't limited to blogging; it borrowed all that past pain as well, and turned it into a kind of perfect storm.

Perhaps of equal concern was the fact that until I became a public theologian and blogger, my faith had always been private or preached behind closed doors.

I had a bold vision for following Jesus right where I lived. I was passionate about Houston and about peace. What I didn't have was the spirituality or community strong enough to sustain a new mission. The difficult thing wasn't the choice to do what I knew was right. The difficult thing was having the inner resources to do what I knew to be right.

More than any generation in human history, we are bombarded with needs and crises. Facebook is a mind-numbing flow of demands, updates, messages, advertisements, news and newsfeeds, wars and rumors of wars all clamoring as if of equal value. While Facebook has mastered the algorithm to feed me what it believes I'm most likely to interact with, it has proven spiritually bankrupt in sorting what I *should* interact with. Everything is presented as equal: cute cats, war in Ukraine, new planetary discovery, friend's brain aneurism or divorce, funny meme, forty million Americans in poverty, quaint Bible verse, first-world rant, Syrian refugees in Texas. All are presented as if on equal ground and are scrolled through lazily on a second screen or while waiting impatiently for a traffic light to turn green.

Kathleen Norris, in her book *Acedia and Me*, speaks candidly about how hard it is to care in the modern age. "We may want to believe that we are still concerned, as our eyes drift from a news anchor announcing the latest atrocity to the NBA scores and stock market quotes streaming across the bottom of the screen. But the ceaseless bombardment of image and verbiage makes us impervious to caring."[1]

In giving myself over to the algorithmic master, I find myself more and more being reformed in its image: an expert at multitasking but impervious to caring.

When I started blogging, I was like many churches that have embraced a missional vision: that is, my mission outpaced the strength both of my identity and of my community. I wonder if our complex world and new vision of discipleship are asking for a new output but are still using the same old hardware to get it. Is it possible for us to live differently if we continue to do the same Christian practices we've always done?

Many of us have an exciting and faithful vision for following Jesus. What we need now are new practices that will sustain us to live into them. In this chapter, we take a look at the second core practice that helps us see and find the gospel next door: forming a disciple-making culture. How can North American Christians pursue a different spirituality and world at the same time?

---

1 Kathleen Norris, *Acedia and Me* (London: Penguin Books, 2008), 129.

WHAT IS A DISCIPLE, AND HOW DO YOU MAKE ONE?

Short of an off-the-shelf curriculum or ten-point how-to guide, here's what I'm coming to believe about becoming disciples. I'm increasingly convinced that the disciple-making culture in Western Christianity is woefully inadequate for equipping us to put our faith into action. Ninety minutes on a Sunday morning or reading a book once a month may make good citizens or church members, but it hasn't proved capable of making faithful disciples. I suspect many of us may feel our caring capacity is limited because we have too much information and too few supporters in our quest for faithfulness. We're trying to do something on our own that was always intended to be lived in community. And not just any community, but a community that exists for others and demonstrates God's alternative to the famine of dominant culture.

The cry of many for a different spirituality is rooted squarely in our realization that our missional calling long ago outstripped our disciple-making capacity. For decades, our mental model of Christian growth has been intertwined with education. We've believed that change occurs when you fill up a person's faith bank with good information.

But becoming a disciple of Jesus is about *formation* far more than *information*. Formation happens in the real world, where you spend the majority of your time, as well as in the practice of the spiritual disciplines. It's a commitment, not a choice. It's a journey deeper into authenticity than any other invitation would fathom.

Like fire in my bones, I believe an abundant life is living life radically with Jesus, and that such a life is possible. I'm learning to see that a disciple is someone who is being transformed while following Jesus as part of a community. I think the actions of disciples include loving our neighbors by serving the poor, the marginalized, and those in need, and by working for the common good to restore individuals, social systems, communities, and nations to God's design.

I also believe you can't podcast yourself to transformation. I don't even believe that we can change. But I do believe that we can *be* changed.

This is at the very heart of Jesus' gospel—the grace of new life in Christ. Grace is spiritual empowerment for missional living, the creative love of God that restores our capacity for goodness in the world.

We'll need a new disciple-making culture, something robust like the early church, something that can divert the inertia in our lives from life-as-expected to life-as-promised.

This book, and every book you've ever read, is just not up to the task—not because of the quality of the books, but because they're *books*. Missional Christians must resist the cultural inertia of learning *about*. Our new faith formation practices will center on learning *to*. Learning *to love*, learning *to act* for justice, learning *to see* our world as it is and can be. Learning *to break and pour* our lives and energies as Jesus broke and poured his love. We are not learning *about* Jesus or doctrine. We are being formed by "*the practices and postures that* I have taught you" so we can "follow the commands I have laid down for you" (Matthew 28:20 The Voice).

We are learning *to be* as Jesus would be if he were us: abundantly alive and consumed with love for our neighbors next door. We are learning *to see* as Jesus sees so that we can love as Jesus loved.

I'm absolutely convinced my friend was right. Without a robust Jesus at the center of our mission and spirituality, we'll be paralyzed. If we don't get Jesus right, we'll be unable to get our mission right.

SPIRITUAL SURGERY

But how can the church do that? What kind of disciple-making practices do we need in order to be formed as Christians who live a Jesus kind of life? What can we do today to become the kind of people who tomorrow do naturally what Jesus asks us to do?

The first step, in order and perhaps importance, is for us to see Jesus as he really is, and not as we want him to be. We must be clear about the uniquely Christian path of becoming fully human and fully alive, and how that differs from culture's path.

My fear of public witness hasn't entirely vanished. I've still got a lot inside me that is resistant to God's love. But my vision is becoming more clear. Joining God on mission is not an after-thought to "real life" or an add-on to Christian living. Joining God on mission is the very heart of Christianity.

But it's not at the center of Western culture. It's so easy to be lured into substituting consumerism or popularity for Jesus' way of being fully human and fully alive; and yet doing so has negative consequences for both me and my city. Like a bowl of spaghetti and sauce, these two views—Western culture and Jesus' way—are nearly impossible to separate once mixed. God's passion for human flourishing invites us to imagine ourselves foremost as followers of the Jesus way and not as citizens of any modern nation. And yet we unwillingly find Christianity mixed with good citizenship, or God's blessing confused with middle-class wealth, or personal success with being where God wants us to be. They're so intermingled we rarely stop to ask if there is another way.

I would say it's not merely that we've blended the two; it's that we've been unable to see that the message of capitalistic con-sumerism is itself a promise of salvation. "Don't worry!" it tells us, "we've got just the thing for that." And whether the "thing" offered is a new Roth IRA, a "get out of jail free (for whites only)" pass, or the right pair of pants, everything seems to have the ability to save us. My favorite example is the Maybelline tagline: "Maybe she's born with it. Maybe it's Maybelline." Just in case you *weren't* born with good looks, Maybelline can make you look like you were.

Are we infected with a Western lifestyle without even knowing it?

Perhaps the most destructive blurring we leave unquestioned is God and country. Overseas missionaries have pointed out the negative effect of collapsing Jesus into Western cultural norms. Historian David Swartz says, "American evangelical imperialism links a valid impulse to spread the Christian gospel with American cultural values such as patriotism, capitalism, and democracy."[2] He shares the story of one Zimbabwean who suggested "the task of making disciples for Jesus Christ was often confused with that of 'civilizing the primitive and savage tribes.'"[3] Who gets to decide what "civilizing" means, anyway? Is it the conception of nuclear families or democracy, or a certain way of dressing or speaking? Or perhaps "civilized" people are those who practice radical hospitality and enemy love?

If we limit gospel to the personal, nonpolitical, and future worlds, nothing theological remains to guide our vision for human community. Without the cultural vision of Christ, it's easy to fill the void with the American dream and assume it to be God's dream. Without Jesus as the model of lifestyle, it's easy to give away our voice to the Democrats or Republicans or the Liberal or Conservative or New Democratic Party, and to trade Christian hope for fear and division. Without the gospel as model, we're prone to allow the government to decide our behavior and not our Lord.

---

2 David Swartz, *The Moral Minority: The Evangelical Left in an Age of Conservatism* (Philadelphia: University of Pennsylvania Press, 2012), 126.
3 Ibid.

Somewhere I've heard surgery called "controlled violence." My heart tells me it's time to commit to the long-term project of surgically separating Jesus' way from the Western way. What other hope do we have? What other hope does our planet have? None that I want to experiment with.

The early Anabaptists called this spiritual surgery *Gelassenheit*. For them, spiritual surgery was both a daily posture and a long-term process of willingly removing all blocks to loving God and neighbor. Anything—theology, tradition, business interests, personal brokenness and shame, God's previous gifts—that prohibits us from following Christ must be removed. Reformer Menno Simons said that Jesus' life-giving invitation is for believers "to suit themselves, in their weakness, to all words, commandments, ordinances, Spirit, rule, example and measure of Christ, as the Scripture teaches; for they are in Christ and Christ is in them."[4] While this spiritual surgery may be sharp as a scalpel, it's also as doggedly committed a process as water eroding rock.

Like Paul, who boldly proclaimed to followers in their imperial capital that "Jesus is Lord!"—and thus that Caesar is *not*—we too must pledge our primary allegiance to Jesus. The good news of the beautiful new world God is re-creating is an alternative and life-sustaining vision different from any other ideas about full humanity. This is why spiritual surgery is not only something we do; it's a gift given. "Do not be conformed to this world, but be transformed by the renewing of your minds, so that you may discern what is the will of God—what is good and acceptable and perfect" (Romans 12:2).

It may be counterintuitive, but pledging sole allegiance to Jesus is the most freeing thing we can do. Sure, it drastically narrows the direction our path can take, but it magnifies our

4 Menno Simons, *The Complete Work of Menno Simon*, vol. 2 (Elkhart, IN: John F. Funk and Brother, 1871), 263.

own potential; it was Jesus himself who said that you "will do greater works than these" (John 14:12).

Talk about something that is hard to believe! And yet there it is, written in the tantalizing red of Jesus' words. "We are invited, expected, and urged to become persons we are not," says Walter Brueggemann. "We are invited, expected, and urged to become mature so that we may assume joyous responsibility over the affairs of the Lord."[5]

Like Peter, whose entire life was expanded when Jesus called him a partner in fishing for people, thrusting him into the public arena in Jerusalem, Antioch, Caesarea, and even Rome. Or Martin Luther King Jr., about whom Ella Baker has said, "The movement made Martin. Martin didn't make the movement." Do you remember the story about Bob and Cathie Baldwin? Their spiritual lives grew exponentially when they decided to get on mission with Jesus and their neighbors next door.

Harriet Tubman, Jim Elliot, Mother Teresa, Teresa of Avila, Dorothy Day: for all their greatness (and they were great!), they were each made household names because living into Jesus' story was a far bigger vision than they could have ever dreamed. My mind is filled with faces for whom this is true. I wonder who you know. Whose life has been forever changed by God's big dreams?

FAITHWALKING 101

I've always been passionate about spirituality. I've been known to lose myself in our church sanctuary for hours of praying or singing, and it's not unusual to find me sloppy-teared weeping in an inconvenient spot like Barnes & Noble, journal in hand. But what I realized the day I started a public writing ministry in Houston is that what had worked for me for so long no longer did.

---

5 Walter Brueggemann, *Peace* (Saint Louis: Chalice Press, 2011), 173.

Actually, that's not exactly right. It's not that my spirituality wasn't working. It was doing exactly what it was designed to do; I just didn't need it to do that anymore. It left me with a sense of certainty but did little to clarify the world I lived in. It challenged my own sin but left me helpless to understand the weightier issues of injustice and the roots of violence. I found myself quite adept at interpreting ancient texts but incapable of interpreting the nightly news. Even as I transitioned from young adult to family man, my spiritual practices and theology were stuck in an outdated college-student mode.

There's a bridge in Honduras that explains this better than I can. Given to Honduras by the people of Japan, the Choluteca Bridge was designed to connect two communities across a river. Built with the finest materials and state-of-the-art design, the bridge withstood even an exceptionally harsh hurricane, Hurricane Mitch, in 1998.

Mitch dropped seventy-five inches of rain in several hours, washing out entire towns, killing more than eleven thousand people, and causing immense infrastructural damage (including the destruction of 150 other bridges). But the Choluteca Bridge did as it was designed to do and remained standing. There was only one problem: Mitch redrew the path of the river and left the bridge standing in the middle of dry land, rendering it completely worthless.

The bridge did what it was designed to do; the world just stopped needing what it offered. The world had changed so drastically that the bridge was irreversibly irrelevant. When I moved to Houston, my faith and my church were like that bridge. But today I know something I didn't know when I moved to Houston in 2008. There is a different model of Christian formation that is forming missional disciples of Jesus.

Started in 2007, Faithwalking is a new way of equipping disciples for mission where we live, work, and play. It was a direct response by several of Houston's key church leaders to the church's growing sense that the new wine Jesus was offering needed new wineskins to hold it. Like many new forms of spiritual formation, Faithwalking is based on the belief that personal transformation happens through the integration of action and reflection, and almost always with others.

We train doctors and athletes by setting them loose to practice a skill and then talking about how it went, what they learned, and what they should do differently in the future. And then they do it all over again, and over and over and over again, until they get it right. This is just good pedagogy. It reminds me of the old saying "I hear and I forget; I see and I remember; I do and I understand."

Through a series of retreats, cohorts, and coaching, Faithwalking uses this same cycle of practice and reflection to form disciples in three core competencies of missional engagement—liberation, learning, and living. In this way of forming faith, the gospel is our teacher and our experience with missional living is the subject.

All of us—even the most faithful among us—are stopped from being fully faithful to Jesus in some aspect of our lives. Faithwalking helps to both name what those blocks are and move us into space where we can find freedom from what hinders us. Personal shame and past decisions we've made to protect ourselves from harm (often unconscious decisions we made as children) hijack our commitment to faithfulness. Thus, one of the primary lessons of this disciple-making culture is the importance of vulnerability, a skill practiced repeatedly as a way of bringing our full selves to God and those we partner with in mission.

In the opening to this chapter I mentioned my fear of "standing out" in ministry. I'd committed to a low-key and out-of-the-limelight ministry. But until I intentionally worked to name and find freedom from that original fear, I was limited in my ability to hear God's call and follow Christ without limits. As a leader of several Faithwalking cohorts over the years, I've witnessed firsthand the power of honesty when it comes to freeing us to live a daily life of discipleship.

But none of this can happen alone, as in previous information-based learning; disciple-making must happen in a committed community of grace and truth. Faithwalking also uses the practice-reflection learning cycle to train us in the skills of co-operative teamwork and healthy relationships. Several of these key skills include learning by listening well, managing anxiety in groups, and empowering groups to face their own integrity gaps by keeping their word. We are a learning community with trusted others with whom we can authentically learn, openly fail, and slowly grow.

The third core competency of Faithwalking is living the life of a disciple in a missional community committed to local issues and the common good. This is not about several one-off service projects, but a long-term commitment to the same people in the same neighborhood through ministry *with* and not *to* neighbors. I've come to expect a certain amount of trial-and-error for missional communities, which need to constantly reflect on how they're showing up and the guiding principles that energize their work. This authentic community becomes a practical incarnation of the alternative lifestyle Jesus longs for all human communities to know.

Check out the clear and compelling vision statement for Faithwalking that captures what that alternative lifestyle looks like.

Faithwalkers are members of a community of disciples of Jesus who are being personally transformed and becoming catalysts for mobilizing Christians to become the functioning body of Christ in their neighborhoods, workplaces, and third places:

- To serve the poor, the marginalized, and those in need
- To work for the common good
- To restore individuals, social systems, communities and nations to God's design.

This purpose drives everything we do. It drives the reason that we are here. And it expresses the hope that we have in Jesus' ability to redeem and restore the places in which we live and work.

Liberation, learning, and living—these are the foundation for one new form of disciple-making culture that is changing the story in and about the church.

Dozens of missional communities and hundreds of Christians are experiencing personal transformation that's leading them to radically put their faith into action. In almost every neighborhood in Houston; in places like Guatemala, New York, Canada, and Colorado; and in denominations like the Reformed Church in America, Faithwalking is making an impact on local communities by changing hearts of folks just like you.

I didn't come to be an active Christian with a bold peace witness and reputation for seeking justice by studying in the Bible that I needed to do those things. I already knew I needed to do those things. I am becoming those things because I have studied my *fear*. I've studied it long enough to understand what it is trying to teach me, studied it deeply enough that I don't flinch at its darkness, and studied it with others who have courageously spoken truth into my life while surrounding me with unexpected grace.

The path of full personhood and healthy spirituality is the path of radically following Jesus in daily life. He is an amazing spiritual detective, the great preacher of peace sent by God in the exact same way we have been sent. To fully understand how Jesus was sent, we need to know the promises he came to fulfill, and God's vision for the messianic age. In the next section we'll look at the Hebrew Bible's clear and compelling mental model of who and how God is in our world: the concept of shalom.

Part III

*The Gospel Gift
of Peace*

*Humankind has not woven
the web of life. We are but one
thread within it. Whatever
we do to the web, we do to
ourselves. All things are bound
together. All things connect.*

—CHIEF SEATTLE

SEVEN

Shalom and the Common Good

IN A SMOKE-FILLED ROOM on the top floor of the Gulf Building, Jesse Jones called a summit.

Houston, like other cities on the brink of the Great Depression in 1929, was threatened with financial ruin, a future Jones refused to accept. "We cannot escape being our brother's keeper," Jones argued to twelve bank, utility, and oil executives. After hours of debate and persuasion, Jones and his team agreed to tackle the crisis together. They would all put the common good above their own interests, pool their resources, and guarantee financial support through the tough times ahead. It was a kind of bank insurance before there was bank insurance.

And it worked. Not a single bank in Houston failed during the Depression. The leaders didn't pass a law or resign themselves to a dog-eat-dog world of corporate competition. They fixed the problem themselves. Both Henry Ford in Detroit and J. P. Morgan in New York City ignored Jones's example, and their cities' banks were devastated. Jones later wrote to Captain James Baker, "None of us had a right not to stop the tragedy."

Jones's influence went well beyond Houston. In his role in the Reconstruction Finances Corporation, he brought the same "common good first" approach to preventing the widespread failure of farms, banks, railroads, and many other businesses on the national level. Jones was passionate about using his day-in and day-out vocation to make Houston a flourishing city for all citizens. His legacy continues through the Houston Endowment.

One generation after Jesse Jones sat in his smoke-filled summit, Rev. William Lawson presided over a meeting of leaders in a similar yet segregated room at the Rice Hotel in downtown Houston. This time the question was racial integration. How could Houston integrate safely and without the violence Birmingham and other cities suffered?

Here, without conflict, force, or fight, it was decided Houston would desegregate in one day. The decision wasn't made on moral grounds. Instead, it was pointed out that Houston was becoming Boomtown USA and that its economic reputation would be stained irreparably by riots and continued racial segregation. NASA, the expansion of the seaport, and the Astrodome—sometimes called the eighth wonder of the world—had all just come to Houston and were altering the world's opinion of the Bayou City.

What was for Lawson a spiritual mandate was for most in the room purely a business decision that led quietly, without fanfare, to desegregating Houston. On an agreed-upon day, the White Only signs simply disappeared. A white child could hop onto a desegregated bus and find himself finally free to sit in the back to look out those huge windows. A black woman could browse in Foley's and even try on that dress that had caught her eye.

Lawson knew this decision was a far cry from liberating Houston from racialization. But having acted in its own self-interest, the business community had joined the conversation and actually helped justice take a large step forward. Both Jones and Lawson used the jobs they had and the time God had given them to create a community with a healthy quality of life. What makes a community healthy, and how can God's people pursue God's answer to that question? If each of our communities were working as designed, what would that mean?

CAMELS EVERYWHERE!

The first chapters of the Bible tell of a garden created by God in perfect harmony. Eden was a land without want or shame built through God's nonviolent creative love.

The authors of Genesis tell our creation story as a stunning inversion of other local myths, which suggested that creation was the product of incredible violence. In these other stories, the slaughter of the gods results in a creation filled with chaos and violent creatures that mimic their gods.

Eden and all the earth are birthed not through slaughter but through the gentleness of the spoken world. God spoke and the world was birthed into being. "Let there be light. . . . Earth, sprout. . . . Lights, come out! . . . Earth, generate life!" (Genesis 1:3, 11, 14, 24 The Voice). In Christian theology, creation is a gift that repudiates not science but violence: the violence of creating things through death.

Later, when death and chaos do take over and shalom is broken, community redevelopment is imagined as restoration of Eden's harmony (Ezekiel 36:22-38; Revelation 22) and the coming of a new messianic community (Isaiah 2, 9, 11, Revelation 21).

Both of these metaphors come complete with big-picture promises and street-level details. And both are centered in God's gift of shalom, freely given.

When the prophets hunt for a single word capable of holding all the promises of God, they return time and again to *shalom*, the word we often translate as "peace." Peace is the Bible's biggest word and the incomprehensibly enormous gift of community flourishing.

It is far more than the absence of violence or the lack of injustice. Instead, shalom points us to something positive in the presence and promises of God. It is our world filled with goodness, not merely empty of evil. Shalom is what the world would look like if we were healthy spiritually, relationally, and in our interactions with creation.

Shalom makes things work. It's as simple as that. Shalom is integrity in community that sustains everything and everyone. We see this in both Eden and its return, in creation and God's re-creation. *Integrity* is one of our great English words with dual meanings, and both speak to the character of shalom.

What may come to mind most quickly is the character trait of people doing what they say they'll do when and how they say they'll do it. But we also like our bridges to have integrity, right? We want to know the bridge taking us across a waterway isn't broken or breaking and that it will continue to work until we're safely to the other side. As in this example, workability is also what we mean when we speak of integrity. Communities with shalom have both integrity and workability.

The ancient prophets save some of their most poetic and specific images to capture shalom. Isaiah could have lectured about his economic plan of growth but instead paints a humorous picture of an overwhelming abundance of camels (Isaiah 60:6). Jeremiah talks about people singing in the streets. Micah mentions "giving up war training *and maneuvers*" (Micah 4:3 The Voice) and, in passing, Malachi says we'll go out leaping like newborn calves (Malachi 4:2). Ezekiel connects the workability of cities with Eden come again. "This land that was desolate has become like the garden of Eden; and the waste and desolate and ruined towns are now inhabited and fortified" (Ezekiel 36:35).

But my favorite is Zechariah's vision of a city "full of boys and girls playing in its streets" (Zechariah 8:5). If a picture speaks a thousand words, these metaphors paint a thousand pictures. What a great image: that my kids can play in the streets of Houston without fear or supervision! Such images remind me of Robert Hodge's dream that the next generation of black artists will be able to paint teacups. What strikes me isn't Zechariah's poetry but the wholesale change required for his vision to become reality. The street-level details need to be in place before these imaginative pictures can become reality. Imagine the workability of your neighborhood if your kids could safely play in the streets or if every one of your neighbors were to run singing past your house.

Two hundred and thirty-five times, the Hebrew Scriptures use this word *shalom* to unpack God's deep caring for every aspect of life and human community. Shalom is love writ large across the streets of our cities and the secrets of our hearts—everywhere, everything, and everyone . . . every, every, every.

Modern nation-states hold this vision for themselves and offer their own synonyms for shalom. The preamble to the U.S. Constitution speaks of "the general welfare of the people" and the Canadian Constitution Act, 1867, proposes "peace, order and good government."

The oft-used contemporary phrase "common good" captures the idea of shalom: that our own welfare is inexplicably intertwined with the health of our community. The prophet Jeremiah tells his people to care for Babylon at every level because their welfare is connected to the city's welfare (Jeremiah 29:7).

Isn't that exactly how Christians are supposed to be known, through our initiating love of one another? The very essence of Jesus' teachings is love. Love as reconciliation, love as forgiveness, love as restoring community, love that breaks down whatever divides us and creates a new alternative community. We love God and self, and in doing so become the kind of people who love our neighbors as if they were us. Hardest of all, we love our enemies.

Paul captures the cultural vision of shalom perfectly: "Get beyond yourselves and protecting your own interests; *be sincere*, and secure your neighbors' interests first" (Philippians 2:4 The Voice). This is the kind of community Jesus created. Shalom is God's cultural vision for a gospel-formed community.

No matter how central to Christian behavior peacemaking may be, it's even more fundamental to Christian theology. The testimony of the early church *increases* the importance of peace for understanding God's actions in our world. To understand God you need to understand peace, and the same is true of understanding the gospel, Jesus, God's kingdom, salvation, evangelism, atonement, and grace.[1]

---

1 God (Romans 15:33; 16:20; 2 Corinthians 13:11; Philippians 4:9; Colossians 3:15; 1 Thessalonians 5:23; 2 Thessalonians 3:16; Hebrews 13:20); Jesus (Ephesians 2; Colossians 1:20); gospel (Acts 10:36; Romans 10:15; Ephesians 2:17; 6:15); kingdom (Romans 14:17); salvation (Romans 5:11; Ephesians 2:11-14); atonement (Ephesians 2; Colossians 1:20); being made right (Romans 5:1); healing (Mark 5:34); spirituality (Romans 8:6; Galatians 5:22; Philippians 4:7; Colossians 3:15); creation (Mark 4:39); the church (Acts 9:31; Ephesians 2); mission (John 20:21; Matthew 5:8; Luke 19:41; Romans 12:14-18; 1 Corinthians 7:15; 2 Corinthians 5:16-21; Hebrews 12:14; 1 Peter 3:11); evangelization (Acts 10:36; Ephesians 2:17); faithful living (Romans 3:17; Luke 19:41; Romans 8:6); and blessing (Luke 24:36; Romans 1:7; 1 Corinthians 1:3).

Like grace, which is the spiritual heartbeat of individual flourishing, shalom is the spiritual heartbeat of community flourishing. It's all the promises of God rolled up into a one-stop-shop word, and it's ours for the taking. The gift of shalom is less about morality and more about theology. It's not about ethics so much as grace. It's not primarily behavior but belief that our God can heal the brokenness of individualism, competition, and the acceptance of inequality.

Shalom is a gift for every size of community, from households to our global family and everything in between. In this chapter we'll explore shalom for our cities, and in chapter 8 we'll look at how shalom connects everything and everyone around the world. But first, let's step outside our front doors for a moment and see what the gospel has to say about our neighborhoods and the cities we call home.

SHALOM THROUGH THE CITY

If the gospel of God is the lens that helps us see the world as it really is, what does the gospel make of Houston? In what ways does Houston work as shalom demands, and in what ways doesn't it work? And how are Christians called to seek the peace of our cities?

In the history of civilization, cities have proven to be pretty amazing inventions. They evoke a kind of timeless sentiment, a psychology of wonder that pulls people near and far. Cities are engines of jobs, quality of life, and incredible opportunity. They tend to be remarkably welcoming to immigrants, extending an open invitation for anyone to come and compete in the marketplaces of ideas and commerce.

Cities create a fusion of people and their ideas that can exponentially increase imagination and production. With their coffee shops and cultural intersections, they're like open-source computer code: available to anyone and everyone to use or change as needed. When people come together, they become more than the sum of their parts. But bringing people together also makes them incredibly frugal and efficient, consuming less than the sum of their parts.

There is obviously something about Houston that is working, given its incredible ability to attract people and generate wealth. Our diversity is unmatched, and folks in Houston are counting down the days until our population surpasses Chicago's, a target we'll likely reach by 2020. Cities are amazing crossroads where God brings the world to the church's doorstep. The magnetic power of cities creates space for the blending of difference that reflects the beauty of creation and the hope for God's people.

For me, all sectors in a community have a God-given purpose. When business works as God intended, commerce contributes. When it doesn't work, you have greed. When education works, children are equipped to work for the common good and are nurtured to grow. When education doesn't work, it becomes bureaucracy and stops meeting children's needs.

The Jones and Lawson stories demonstrate how ordinary people use their vocational gifts and their cities to spread shalom. When our communities are working well, Christians can use cities themselves to further the common good of shalom. We can advocate for humane policies and programs that meet the basic needs of all our neighbors. The Houston branch of Food Not Bombs, for example, is a local nonprofit that has used this method to overturn a city ordinance prohibiting sharing food with the homeless.

Workable cities also mean we can use our jobs and vocations to improve the economic livability of our cities.

WHAT'S THE BOTTOM LINE: THE MARKET OR THE PEOPLE?

Every day, the privilege of city life reminds me how well Houston works for me. That's not the question; clearly cities work for some. The question is whether they work for everyone, or only for an intentional few.

Like most North American cities, Houston is a market city, driven by market concerns. Nearly everything that happens here is tied to the production of wealth. Remember how both Jones and Lawson reached their goals by catering to the corporate world's bottom line? That's how we tend to think about making progress. We build parks to attract young professionals and expand our freeways so the well-off few, like me, have ease of access to the opportunities of the city.

The problem in a city like Houston is that so few of our resources are given to the people who are already here, especially the most vulnerable, and are instead invested in future growth. And countless people fall through the cracks we've chosen to live with. Our primary working assumption is an individualism that accepts inequality. We've agreed that some jobs are more valuable than others, that some deserve wealth and others less than a living wage.

Texas is one of the most religious states in the country. Yet Texas consistently ranks in the lowest tier of states in addressing childhood poverty and providing health insurance for children (we rank dead last), mental health expenditures for children (ranked second to last), and education expenses per student.[2] Several other embarrassing quality-of-life rankings for our children support this picture as well.

A full quarter of the students living in my county live in poverty. In 2009, half the children in Texas were living in

---

2. Jennifer Riley, "Report: Top 10 Most Religious States in America," *Christian Post*, February 2, 2009, http://www.christianpost.com/news/report -top-10-most-religious-states-in-america-36746/.

low-income families, compared with 42 percent nationally. This means that nearly half our children are set up to be unsuccessful. The long-term risks associated with child poverty go well beyond learning on an empty stomach; children living in poverty have a higher risk of dropping out of school, of poor adolescent health, of poor employment outcomes, and of experiencing poverty as adults.

In a statement that could only arise in a market economy, Rick Santorum said he believes that income inequality is essential to shalom and American society. "There is income inequality in America. There always has been and hopefully, and I do say that, there always will be," Santorum said to a group of Detroit business leaders in 2012. "Why? Because people rise to different levels of success based on what they contribute to society and to the marketplace, and that's as it should be."[3]

Houston today stands as the all-American market city, comfortable with the inequities that drive growth and separate our communities. We hold this assumption so strongly we might not even be aware of an alternative. Oilmen take billions from the ground and give millions back to communities. Sure, our friendly business environment provides incredible resources for charity. But does it also create the need for charity in the first place?

One of the most creative responses to this tear in Houston's fabric of shalom is the Project Curate restaurant incubator. More than charity and something different from a traditional business model, it's a fantastic blending of them both.

The ministry of Project Curate is simple: create jobs for women who have suffered abuse and equip them for life in the workforce. But the way the organization plans to pull this off is what's interesting. They have brought Christian investors and

---

3 Quoted in Holly Ellyatt, "Income Inequality: Is It Good for Everyone?" CNBC, January 8, 2013, http://www.cnbc.com/id/100361302.

restaurant experts together on an abandoned piece of property in Houston's Museum District. There they intend to set up a series of food truck–type pods, in which the women can be trained in restauranteering and earn a living wage.

Time and some resources will be donated. But this will be a business able to stand on its own two feet and to give back to the community. Project Curate's approach is to blend vocation and volunteerism, and embrace both charity and justice in the pursuit of the common good. What I love the most about the organization's work is the equal and cooperative work of all involved. This is ministry that happens *with* those in need, not *to* those in need. And it's a longer-term commitment than a one-off service project—a core distinction for neighborhood mission.

Incubating jobs in a charity-driven business redeems what the market economy offers. But it does so by creating alternative communities that prophetically model a people-centered way of being. Beyond acts of charity toward individuals, justice creates patterns of behavior, systems of community, and relational interactions so that there is no longer a need for acts of charity. If a ministry of mercy would feed the poor through a food pantry, a ministry of justice would explore the systemic reasons why poverty exists in the first place and then seek to change the system so poverty is no more.

VOCATION AS MISSIONAL ENGAGEMENT

Twila gave herself completely to her vocation as a teacher. She loved her work, her students, and the deep-rooted feeling that teaching in a public school was exactly what God had called her to do. Well before she'd ever heard the word *missional* uttered by a preacher, she had joined God in mission at Valley Oaks Elementary in Houston.

This was her expression of faith and creative way of seeking the peace of our city. And she was good at it, too, for decades. She not only taught with excellence but also cared for coworkers, was known for her nonanxious presence, and prayed daily for her students.

But her efforts didn't fit the mental model of being a "good Christian," which meant, in her setting, volunteering at church above and beyond time spent at work. "It was always as if what I did didn't matter to the church," she said. "Unless I volunteered or joined a committee, I always felt the church didn't count what I did. The pressure was always to do more at church."

This story helps me understand how we think about mission. As a pastor who regularly invites volunteers to serve the church, I find Twila's story a needed challenge.

For hundreds of years, the mission of the church has been thought about in this way: special people do special things for God, and everybody else supports it financially. We call and ordain pastors to be these special people who do special things when they live at home, and we commission missionaries for the same work that happens to be "over there." For the rest of us, "being Christian" and connecting to God's story happens primarily through tithing and volunteerism.

Here's another example of putting our vocation to work for the common good. Jerry Galder is an executive at a local marine transportation corporation called Kirby Corporation. He's part of a group of about a hundred Christians there who believe that being faithful witnesses can go beyond Bible studies and prayer ministry to include the actual work that they do in their vocations. They regularly ask themselves two questions: What is God's intention for this corporation? And how do we help Kirby Corporation use its influence for the common good?

When hurricanes hit the Gulf Coast, Kirby Corporation regularly uses its disaster strike teams for disaster relief. Scores of Kirby volunteers have gone up and down the coast serving Kirby families and their neighbors. They use their vocational gifts for the common good.

Closer to home, Jerry and his group influenced their company to encourage employees in their main office to leave work for two hours a week, with pay, and go to nearby Cloverleaf Elementary to serve as mentors. That's the end game for us: people following Jesus not where their church building is but right where they already are. It's about equipping Christians to participate in God's mission first and in church activities second.

ENGAGING THE CULTURE OF THE WORLD

But cities, no less than people, have fallen victim to sin and the consequences of the fall. Sometimes because of this the church stands for values in sharp opposition to North American culture, and needs to model entirely different ways of being.

Cities need redemption. And God has given our cities cultural models for how they are intended to be in the church. The question for the church today is how to bring the cultural vision of life we call the gospel to engage the cultural vision of life the world holds.

One of the fundamentals of the missional movement is missional communities. The church isn't on mission primarily as a bunch of individuals who are out to spread the gospel one person at a time. We're an alternative community declaring and demonstrating the gospel's new vision for community through incarnational ministry of table and casserole, through caring and just ministry. The church is a countermovement whose nature is different and nonconformed, and it behaves curiously before the watching world. We are part of the gospel, part of what God is doing in the world, and part of how God does it.

Missional communities are modeled after the ancient concept of the *ecclesia*. In ancient Greece, all communities had an ecclesia made up of community leaders who gathered to discern what was best for their people. These weren't religious bodies, and yet, out of all the vocabulary choices for religious community, the early church began to see itself in this unique way. I love this image. It challenges us to see our ministry as discerning what's best for our neighborhoods; as Christians, we do so by seeing them through a gospel lens. Ecclesia are smaller in size than congregations and function in direct ways to evangelize peace and restore the wholeness to systems, souls, and streets. As I've experienced them, they are usually a group of five to twelve people. They do not *replace* the congregation but are models of the life and love of Christ to certain communities.

Houston includes incredible missional communities in nearly every neighborhood and every sector of the city. People are sharing commitment to mentoring in schools, overcoming poverty in neighborhoods, providing adequate jobs, creating community in isolated apartments, working to abolish the death penalty, and feeding the homeless healthy meals.

The Fifth Street missional community demonstrates to their neighbors in southwest Houston what life is like in God's kingdom. What I love about their story is that they don't see themselves as service providers but as a group of Christians whose culture is itself a gift. They've rooted themselves in a neighborhood that looks and feels forgotten. Poverty-stricken, ignored by landlords, and refused resources that the wealthier members of the city receive, the homes on this street are practically thrown on top of one another so that landlords can get all the money they can.

This is a hard neighborhood to know where to start. The problems seem so overwhelming. But you have to start doing something. God's gospel of shalom helped those in the Fifth Street community know what shape their ministry should take.

The Fifth Street missional community has set up mentoring programs for neighborhood children and works with government agencies and nonprofits to provide resources to the underserved. Through their vocations and volunteering, the members address the brokenness of their community in every way they can.

But what's special about the Fifth Street missional community is that they are not alone. It's not that they are several lights of the world working side by side; they're the light together: a single gift, a gospel-formed culture, a sign and foretaste of what is to come and is now here, a demonstration of God's plan for human community. Knowing that the brokenness of their community was cultural, their response was cultural, too. They are engaging the culture of the world with the alternative culture of Jesus.

The new lifestyle of Jesus is modeled in dozens of ways. The Fifth Street team is committed to working together, loving their neighbors, and learning whatever skills they need to do it.

They've discovered that when people get out of their churches and into action, it gives their neighbors hope. Theirs is a huge story to tell about God's redeeming work. They believe that if their neighborhood were functioning as designed, it would be filled with college graduates and children playing in the streets. And so they live today in the gap as partners with God in seeking the shalom of the place they live and love.

Shalom happens in endlessly creative ways in cities around the world—through vocation and volunteerism, individual efforts and group efforts. What would your city or neighborhood look and feel like if it were filled with shalom? How is your city both part of and block to God's intentions for all its people? Is it possible the health of your city is tied to your vocation and willingness to volunteer your time?

EIGHT

Three Trillion Dollars of Potholes

WAR HAS A WAY of making the world feel small.

Several years after I joined Twitter, I stumbled across an Israeli bombing invasion of Gaza happening in real time. Mahmoud, a Palestinian dad, began tweeting when the apartment next to his was leveled to the ground, sending him and his three-year-old son under the table for cover. Before any news outlets picked up the story, I was in a Panera, coffee in hand, communicating with Mahmoud. I listened to his horrifying updates and offered prayers for this Muslim brother.

It reminded me of the night the first Gulf War began with "smart" bombs and Tomahawk missiles raining down on Iraq in 1991. I watched the war unfold with no media mention of Iraqi families like Mahmoud's, who were undoubtedly collateral damage. That night I felt hollow, and promised I'd never again pledge my allegiance to any flag or anyone other than God.

Now here I was again with a front-row seat to more war, this time without media censor or the innocence of youth. Baghdad and Gaza were war zones in far-off places. But I was reminded again how short the distance between "here" and "there" can be. In fact, during the Cold War, our addiction to violence nearly brought nuclear devastation to Texas.

In the last week of October 1958, the United States and the former Soviet Union agreed to a temporary halt in nuclear testing. Days later, when the USSR detonated several bombs near Kuykengol, Kazakhstan, seven miles in the air, President Eisenhower called off the test halt.

Some sixty-six hundred miles away, on November 4, 1958, a B-47 bomber took off from Dyess Air Force Base in Abilene, Texas. Armed at all times with live ammunition and nuclear weapons, the plane was integral to the country's nuclear hedge of protection against the perceived Soviet nuclear threat. The strato-fortress jet exploded immediately after takeoff, landing in Edgar Davis's field a half mile from Butterfield Elementary School, causing a nonnuclear detonation of a nuclear bomb. The explosion left a crater thirty-five feet wide and six feet deep.

It could have been a full-on nuclear explosion. It wasn't. But it did take fifty-four years until the Texas Commission on Environmental Quality deemed the contaminated land totally clean. Decades-long cleanup is not unusual when our bombs go astray. The United States is still cleaning up the former tomato fields of Palomares, Spain, where two of our nukes spewed radioactive materials over a huge swath of land when they were accidentally dropped fifty years ago.

Texas has had its share of brushes with accidental nuclear catastrophe. On May 22, 1957, an El Paso flight accidentally dropped one of the largest nukes ever made out of the plane's cargo bay. And a building full of nuclear components caused a massive explosion at Lacklund Air Force Base in San Antonio just a few days before President Kennedy was shot in Dallas.

During the Cold War, the United States lost—as in, they're still out there somewhere—eight or more nukes, including in a bog in North Carolina, in the Mediterranean, in the Pacific Ocean eighty miles off the Japanese coastline, and under the ice-cap of Greenland. For a ten-year period during the height of the Cold War, the United States had the equivalent of five thousand Hiroshima bombs in the air every second of the day—mostly in secret flight patterns over Canada and other countries.[1]

Has anything made our world feel smaller than the threat of nuclear annihilation? A world so small that one city-killing weapon in 1945 grew to such monstrous proportions we soon found ourselves talking of nation killing, and inevitably species extinction.

Politics, as the saying goes, really is all local. Globalization has brought the world to our doorstep and has expanded our footprint to the world. What happens out there and far away affects the lives of our neighbors next door. The reverse is also true: decisions we take for granted change the lives of neighbors far away.

Canadian scientists joined Americans in Los Alamos to develop a weapon which "left the civilized world dumbfounded," said the Quebec newspaper *L'Autorité*. One man speaks, and the United States becomes the only country to intentionally and unapologetically target hundreds of thousands of civilians with nuclear weapons of mass destruction.

Things as basic to our lifestyle as out-of-season tomatoes, cheap, fashionable clothing, and corn subsidies all signal that we are living in a global community the likes of which no

---

1 See L. Douglas Kenney, *15 Minutes: General Curtis LeMay and the Countdown to Nuclear Annihilation* (London: St. Martin's Griffin, 2012), 209; and "8 Nuclear Weapons the U.S. Has Lost," http://mentalfloss.com/article/17483/8-nuclear-weapons-us-has-lost.

generation before ours could imagine. When the cell phone I use every day transitioned from luxury item to essential gadget, women and children in the Democratic Republic of Congo suffered extreme violence related to the mining of its essential minerals. And the list goes on.

We are one global community who shares this one blue planet. But as a Christian, one thing is becoming ever more clear for me. The gospel, far more than war, should make our world feel small.

THE GLOBAL GIFT OF SHALOM

I confess I have not always understood the gift and responsibility of being the one body of Christ on earth.

Before I lived in Houston, I lived in Oregon with the trees. They were everywhere, towering above the valleys and mountains, and I loved them dearly. One in particular caught my eye and gave me a deep sense of self-understanding. It was a lone, strong tree standing proudly for all to see atop the highest hill around. I would point it out to friends and talk about the meaning I'd given it. That tree symbolized everything I wanted to be—strong in the storms of life, a model of independence, and noticeable on life's horizon.

It was many years later that I realized the meaning I'd given that tree was actually a lie. I'm not a lonely tree fighting for survival out in the middle of nowhere. I was young and foolish to think as much—just as it's foolish to believe a woman can be an island, individuals build companies, or that Neil Armstrong made it to the moon alone. That tree isn't what I look like at my best but at my most vulnerable.

I've started to see myself in another equally striking image: the image of the earth rising over the moon's horizon. There are various versions of this image, all taken by astronauts looking out over the 238,000 miles from the moon back to earth.[2] The image itself is stunningly blue, dangling just out of the reach of poetry to capture it or the mind's ability to understand its greatness.

This is an image that tells the truth about human existence. It invites us to imagine the entire community of creation as one pale blue dot orbiting the sun in a galaxy filled with suns, which is itself one of some hundred billion galaxies in our universe. What strikes me most profoundly when I see the earthrise pictures is that the earth from space has no borders. Unlike a tree without a forest, the earthrise image celebrates the central truth that God so loved the world . . . the whole world, our shared world, the only world we have. God's love for the world includes all people and all cultures.

The globalization of the gospel is at the very heart of God's plan, which Jesus came to reveal—"to gather up all things in him, things in heaven and things on earth" (Ephesians 1:10). This has been God's hope since the moment the fabric of shalom was torn from Eve and her family in Eden.

This mystery is so life-changing that Paul prays for power so we can comprehend "the love of Christ that surpasses knowledge, so that you may be filled with all the fullness of God" (Ephesians 3:18-19). The love that God has for me is a holistic, pulsating, thriving, living, breathing love that encompasses all I am and all I am connected to.

Shalom is God's global gift of love for the whole world, demonstrated by the borderless body of Christ as a new way of being human community. The ancient prophets imagined a time when the world would live in this new way of radical trust. Isaiah said we can trust God deeply enough to transform our weapons into tools and burn our war garments; we simply won't need either anymore. And when he speaks of the messianic promise, he

2 See "Earthrise," *Wikipedia*, last modified January 4, 2016, https://en .wikipedia.org/wiki/Earthrise.

gives a stunning image of trusting God with such ferocity we can live without enemies—"the wolf shall live with the lamb" (Isaiah 11:6). This is the world as it is meant to be. This is the world Jesus was committed to bringing. Through word and work Jesus unraveled violence, creating a new culture in the midst of the old. But his was a message rooted in an ancient path.

In the opening pages of the Bible, we learn that God looked at his world and saw that it was good. Turn to the last page, and we read that God is making all things new. Not all *new things*, as if God must wipe out human history as we know it and start again. But that God is making a beautiful new world out of the stuff of the old. And in between the moments of creation and re-creation God is restoring all things—things on earth and things in heaven. Mark Labberton, president of Fuller Theological Seminary, says, "God loves the whole world and that encompasses loving us individually. He doesn't love us individually until he ends up loving everyone. The difference is significant because the second order shows the influence of our individualistic American subculture instead of the God who made heaven and earth."[3]

Christians aren't drawn closer to one another through TV and smart bombs; we're closer than flesh-and-blood relatives because we are Christ's body on earth. God's mission is massive and moves beyond even the church's borders; as Isaiah says, "As My servant you will do even more than this, even more than restoring Jacob's family to Me and making Israel right with Me again. I will make you a light for the nations, and You will illumine them until My salvation reaches to the ends of the earth" (Isaiah 49:6 The Voice).

God's restoration is not just for humans but for all creation. John, Paul, and the author of Hebrews all connect Jesus to both

---

3 Mark Labberton, *The Dangerous Act of Worship: Living God's Call to Justice* (Downers Grove, IL: InterVarsity Press, 2012), 80.

creation and re-creation, broadening the scope of salvation from the four chambers of our hearts to the four corners of the planet and our cities.

I've talked about the gospel's ability to help us see our world as it truly is. If we look at the world through the lens of shalom, what will we see? How will shalom help us triage the complexity of life in the twenty-first century? How does it help us understand the gospel that Jesus came preaching?

IN GUNS WE TRUST

If shalom is the promise of healthy relationships with God and others, we've got a head start in understanding what broken shalom will look like. Anything that alienates us from deep reliance on God, and anything that divides humanity, is a sign of broken shalom.

For instance, we can likely all agree we live in an open-carry, mass-shooting, war-habituated world. What's harder to agree on is whether any or all three of those qualities are good.

I suppose it depends on whom you ask. Mass shootings are easy to condemn when they happen in unguarded schools or churches. But what about the mass shooting of Pakistani and Yemeni families by drone warfare? When President Truman killed two Japanese cities, he claimed it was an act of peace, a way out of the war, and a safeguard against Allied deaths. The world's reaction to the same event was one of horror, as was their reaction to our party-line justification. They saw the "earthquake" bomb as a Frankenstein monster sent straight from hell and harnessed by the devil himself. For many in Japan, it was simply known as "the Christian bomb."

During the Cold War, the United States spent $9 trillion erecting a nuclear deterrent similar to Rome's cross to keep an uneasy peace through mutually assured destruction.

That's a nine with twelve zeroes behind it—nine thousand billion dollars.

Today the United States allocates more money to military spending than the next nine or ten countries combined.[4] The U.S. president spends $1 million a minute in a misguided attempt to make peace through war, and does so with money ironically imprinted with the phrase "In God we trust." That seems like a lot of money for a country that claims to trust in God, not guns. In perhaps his most important speech, "Beyond Vietnam," Martin Luther King Jr. connected defense spending to the United States being "the greatest purveyor of violence in the world today."[5]

The author of Revelation asked us to trust in God, saying, "Salvation belongs to our God who is seated on the throne, and to the Lamb!" (Revelation 7:10). When he wrote those words a generation after Jesus, he wasn't saying Jesus was God but not Vishnu, or Jesus and not Allah. He meant something far more disruptive. He meant that God, *not empire*, is the source of human salvation.

This wasn't particularly new for the Bible, which repeatedly uses religious language to talk about military buildup. For example, the psalmist says, "Some take pride in chariots, and some in horses, but our pride is in the name of the Lord our God" (Psalm 20:7). The whole business of empire making and standing militaries was soundly criticized as "a rejection of My rule" over the people (1 Samuel 8:7 The Voice).

Critiquing empire wasn't a sideshow for the early church; it was central to the gospel's cultural vision. When it comes to faith, we've got competing gospels to choose from: Caesar's empire or Jesus' kingdom; the military's nuclear shield or God's hedge of protection. Paul makes his choice clear, proclaiming for those in the imperial capital to hear: "I am not ashamed of the gospel" (Romans 1:16).

Would it not be possible, perhaps even likely, that believing in something other than salvation from God would cause a spiritual crisis in the land? Isaiah was so sure God was trustworthy in the face of lethal force that he sent the sign of Immanuel to prove it. When the king refused to trust God, it became devastatingly clear that spiritual and political crises were the fruit of his unbelief (Isaiah 7). The twentieth century's most beloved American saint, Martin Luther King Jr., certainly believed this was so for us. In the same speech, he said, "A nation that continues year after year to spend more money on military defense than on programs of social uplift is approaching spiritual death."[6]

Some would say that the collapse of Christianity in Europe since the two world wars is indeed a kind of spiritual death. For those who perceive Christianity as having had a role in Europe's destruction, perhaps it is even a welcome death. But this slow spiritual death seems to have even earlier roots. Many in the Enlightenment blamed religion for the medieval wars that devastated Europe. A move away from religion—toward science and reason—was for them a move toward the common good.

The same is true in North America, where the percentage of churchgoers declines every year. Gone are the days when we can assume that everyone in our neighborhood is either a Christian or a lapsed churchgoer. Folks in the West have lost confidence in the ability of the Christian story to make meaning or change.

The violence and arrogance of Western Christianity has left our reputation tattered. We've too often been seen as a

6 Ibid.

laughingstock by outsiders, who watch, bewildered and contemptuous, as we refuse or are unable to do what Jesus asked us to do. The wars of the twentieth century have deteriorated the church's reputation even further. We repeatedly allow something other than God in Christ to determine our behavior. Instead of modeling an alternative culture, we mimic that of our "enemy."

One example is more than enough to illustrate why this may be so. In the 1940s, the Urakami Cathedral in Nagasaki was the largest Catholic institution in East Asia and the center of Japanese Catholic life. The church was filled on the morning of August 9, 1945, as the Catholic community woke up expecting the Feast of the Assumption. While worshipers gathered, American Catholic pilots—along with Fat Man, a plutonium-core atomic weapon of mass destruction—were blessed by their Christian chaplains.

When the lives of these two Catholic communities intersected, the bomb's explosion utterly destroyed the Urakami Cathedral, the heat wave turning all the worshipers inside to ash. Need we wonder why the church's reputation is in question? Seventy years later the myths of Nagasaki's necessity live on, unchallenged and unrepented. We, like Caiaphas before us, have turned over tens of thousands of our brothers and sisters in Christ for execution in a misguided effort to keep the peace for us and ours. Jesus predicted a time such as this when the betrayal and hate of Christians against one another would lead to a crushing spiritual crisis (Matthew 24:10-12).

I am not one to welcome or celebrate spiritual death. I don't believe that what is dying a slow death is Christianity at all, but a very specific civil religion that drapes the cross in a flag and confuses patriotism with God's destiny. There's even a certain sadness about this, as it will mean the loss of institutions and respect. Perhaps, in letting die a kind of Christianity that supports mass death, we'll discover afresh that God is far greater than the West has presumed. Perhaps we'll also be free to explore pacifism as the greatest testimony to the sovereignty of God that the world has ever seen.

Again from King:

> Hardly anything has revealed the pathetic irrelevancy of the church in present-day world affairs as its stand on war. In the midst of a world gone mad with arms buildups, chauvinistic passions, and imperialistic exploitation, the church has stood by, either endorsing these activities or remaining appallingly silent. A weary world, pleading desperately for peace, has often found the church morally sanctioning war.[7]

THE EFFECTS OF WAR ON HOUSTON

Brian is one example of this spiritual crisis we're experiencing. I met him as I was shopping for beach toys with my kids. Homeless since his return from a second tour of duty overseas, Brian asked me if I could buy him a small amount of food. His story is typical of the more than sixty-two thousand veterans in the United States who are homeless on any given night.

According to the Center for American Progress, "the challenges that confront our service members and veterans before, during, and after deployments, from combat stress injuries to unemployment" are a heavy burden.[8] The institute classifies these problems into four main areas: employment, mental health, homelessness, and addiction.

---

7 Martin Luther King Jr., *The Papers of Martin Luther King, Jr.*, series ed. Clayborne Carson, vol. 6, *Advocate of the Social Gospel September 1948–March 1963*, vol. ed. Susan Carson, Susan Englander, Troy Jackson, Gerald L. Smith (Berkley: University of California Press, 2007), 499.

8 Center for American Progress, "Honoring Our Veterans in 2011," November 10, 2011, https://www.americanprogress.org/issues/security/news/2011/11/10/10609/honoring-our-veterans-in-2011/.

As if all this weren't enough, there's the issue of what has come to be known as *moral injury*. Lieutenant Colonel Dave Grossman of the Killology Research Group says, "Killing requires training because there is a built-in aversion to killing one's own kind."[9] If this is true, then all our veterans have been trained in an act that is unnatural. Upward of 90 percent of our returning veterans are willing and able to shoot and kill. You might think that's to be expected; it's their job to do that, right?

But consider this: only 15 percent of World War II veterans "could bring themselves to fire at an exposed enemy soldier." By the Korean War we'd trained our soldiers differently, with the number rising to 55 percent. By the Vietnam War the number was 90 percent, where it hovers today.

So when the Department of Veterans Affairs lists moral injury as a "heavy burden" veterans may carry—a burden that may hurt soldiers when they are either the victims or the perpetrators of trauma—we start to see the full impact of what we have asked of these men and women. The very act of doing what we ask them to do can perpetuate unimaginable problems at home. Theirs is an impossible burden to bear. For Brian, it was a burden that twisted his mind and left him in constant suffering from posttraumatic stress disorder (PTSD). His trauma was so great it spread to those he loved the most, and affected his children with what doctors call secondary PTSD. This, finally, is what pushed Brian out of the house and into the streets, leaving him homeless and disconnected from his family.

Roughly 732,000 citizens of the Houston metro region are dependents of war veterans. Given this fact, we have provided a shaky foundation upon which to build the peace of our city.

---

9 Lt. Col. Dave Grossman, "Trained to Kill," *Christianity Today*, August 10, 1998, available at http://www.killology.com/print/print_trainedtokill.htm.

The war Brian fought in cost $3 trillion, nearly all of which was paid for on credit and not, as many assume, as part of the annual military budget.[10] This doesn't include lost business revenue or production, nor does it account for the tens of thousands of work hours lost by sending civilian soldiers away from their first-responder jobs (an estimated cost of $1 trillion). Nor does this estimate tally losses associated with the fact that one in three veterans with PTSD remain incapable of work.

To comprehend the sheer magnitude of the effect war has on real lives and programs, consider this: the city of Houston's share of the U.S. wars abroad since 2001 is roughly $17.25 billion. For the same amount, we could have offered 18,873 students a full-ride scholarship to university, plus paid 8,539 teachers for ten years, plus covered the cost of Head Start for 71,060 students—combined. We could have wiped out our city's $3.2 billion pension debt more than five times, with a couple of billion dollars to spare.[11]

Potholes: just imagine all the potholes we could have filled with $3 trillion. The enormity of our defense spending has left our schools floundering and our infrastructure deteriorating, and caused our anxiety to skyrocket. To be fair, we've turned war spending and local cuts into a habitual pattern. This was certainly true in President Reagan's multibillion dollar arms race against the Soviets.

And King saw this a generation ago; it's why he began to speak so prophetically against the Vietnam War later in his career. While we ultimately lost the Vietnam War, King believed that it did succeed in defeating one thing: the war on poverty. The country's antipoverty effort was "broken and eviscerated as if it were some idle political plaything of a society gone mad

---

10 Linda J. Bilmes and Joseph Stiglitz, *The Three Trillion Dollar War: The True Cost of the Iraq Conflict* (New York: W. W. Norton, 2008).

11 See the National Priorities Project website, https://www.nationalpriorities .org/interactive-data/trade-offs/?state=48&program=32&place=4835000.

on war who continued to draw men and skills and money like some demonic, destructive suction tube."[12]

As a public theologian, I address the famine in our land from a distinctly Christian perspective. The Houston Committee for Youth and Non-Military Opportunities takes a more practical approach by presenting youth with career options besides the military. Members now take literature racks to every school in the largest school districts in Houston and attend career fairs to speak with youth in an unbiased way about their options. This is a simple action, but one that has had far-reaching impact on the youth of our city.

CUSTODIANS OF CREATION

God's gift of shalom is for all life, and includes peace with God, ourselves, others, and creation itself. Just as shalom reveals the global effect of war on our communities, it also makes clear the effect our everyday choices have on our global neighbors and on the planet where we live. Creation care is to shalom what evangelism is to grace—the Christian's way of loving our neighbor.

Few religious leaders in the world today are as prophetic in their insistence to love our global neighbors as Pope Francis I and Archbishop Desmond Tutu of South Africa. Both have recently tied consumption in the West to a climate catastrophe for the poorest of our global neighbors. More important than the science or moral message is how they tie neighbor care to creation care.

In his inaugural address in 2013, Pope Francis said, "To protect creation is to protect every man and every woman, to look upon them with tenderness and love, to open up a horizon of hope; it is to let a shaft of light break through the heavy clouds;

---

12 King, "Beyond Vietnam."

it is to bring the warmth of hope!"[13] His passion to sustain ecology for the sake of humanity is one of the reasons he chose to be the first pope named after Saint Francis of Assisi.

His time in office has only increased his passion for ecology. In 2015, Pope Francis wrote the first papal encyclical on climate change, called *Laudato Si'*, where he says climate change "represents one of the principal challenges facing humanity in our day" and is connected to a "scandalous level of consumption in some privileged sectors."[14]

Archbishop Tutu is equally passionate about reversing environmental catastrophe in poor communities across the globe, and wrote in 2014 that "we need an apartheid-style boycott to save our planet" from climate change. He put Houston, Texas—otherwise known as the Petro Metro—squarely in the center of his target.[15] And no, Tutu is not talking about the effects of climate change on Houston. He's talking about the causes of climate change and how to bring them to a stop in part through our Christian call to love.

I'm tempted to declaw Tutu's sharp words. After all, I have friends, church members, and neighbors who work in the energy sector. Here, I think, is a case of values colliding. Who was it who said the hardest thing in life isn't the battle between good and evil but the battle between two goods?

Jobs, power, technology, science, and innovation are all good. So are the living wages that come with energy-sector

13 Pope Francis I, "Homily of Pope Francis" (inaugural address, Vatican City, March 19, 2013), http://w2.vatican.va/content/francesco/en/homilies/2013/documents/papa-francesco_20130319_omelia-inizio-pontificato.html.

14 Pope Francis I, "Encyclical Letter *Laudato Si'* of the Holy Father Francis on Care for Our Common Home," May 24, 2015, par. 23 and 172, http://w2.vatican.va/content/francesco/en/encyclicals/documents/papa-francesco_20150524_enciclica-laudato-si.html.

15 Desmond Tutu, "We Need an Apartheid-Style Boycott to Save the Planet," *Guardian*, April 10, 2014, http://www.theguardian.com/commentisfree/2014/apr/10/divest-fossil-fuels-climate-change-keystone-xl.

jobs. But good too are clean air and water, concern for the most vulnerable victims of climate change, and passing on a sustainable legacy to our children.

The wider I spin out Christ's central concern of loving pretty much everyone, the more I'm nudged to see the intersections of creation care and neighbor care. How can I tithe to foreign missions as an act of Christian love and yet live a lifestyle that imperils the very people I'm seeking to serve? How can I put profits above people or corporations above compassion?

Climate disruptions are also increasingly becoming the roots of violence. Climate change led to the 2006–9 drought in Syria, which saw two hundred thousand people die of hunger-related illnesses. The drought forced another one and a half million Syrians to move to cities, where they joined three and a half million Iraqi refugees forced from their homes during both of our wars there.

This climate-conflict cycle is one root of the chaos we see in the Middle East today, including the rise of ISIS. We've also witnessed this climate-conflict cycle in Sudan and Somalia, with similarly devastating results. Perhaps this is why Pope Francis invites all in the church to "hear both the cry of the earth and the cry of the poor."[16]

THE UNINTENDED CONSEQUENCES OF CHOCOLATE

Family friends Kathryn and Dave Bauchelle are anything but preachy radicals. Theirs is a simple story, really. They've heard about neighbors in need, and they've worked to find the best ways to help them out. As it turns out, their neighbors often live half a world away. When it comes to the enormous plight of the poor and the planet, it's incredibly hard to know where to start. They're not always sure what the best thing to do is, but they know they're called to do something.

---

16 Pope Francis I, *Laudato Si'*, par. 49.

They've turned their lifestyle and consumption patterns into a tangible way of loving their global neighbors. In an act of Christian love that baffles many in Houston, they've chosen to share one car between themselves. In a freeway-centered city, this is a bit of an inconvenience to them at times, but they believe it's worth it to save the planet's resources.

The Bauchelles have filled their daily action with small acts of kindness. They use a clothesline instead of a clothes dryer, never use disposable plastic, and buy recyclable paper products when available.

The Bauchelles would be the first to tell you that these cutbacks make only a small impact on a global-scale problem. And yet it is what *they* can do. They are, after all, only responsible for themselves. These acts have another function as well, though—perhaps one more important than their material impact. Each small step reminds them that they are part of a global community. Every tiny decision becomes an act of faith, a decision to become the kind of people who love their global neighbors.

The Bauchelles have energized my family, always encouraging us to do what we can for now. Most impressive is the impact they've had on their workplaces and on our church. Thanks to their education and encouragement, Houston Mennonite Church has begun working intentionally to be more ethical in our consumption. We've studied to understand our part in these problems. Over time we've increasingly embraced fair trade while working to live in environmentally friendly ways.

Our congregation has committed to using only green power and recycled paper products. We buy all our coffee directly from the mother of one of our members, a decision that channels more income to the actual growers. And for several years now we've operated our own not-for-profit fair-trade store—a large cupboard replenished weekly with the most popular fair-trade items our members request, including soap, coffee, and chocolate.

Buying fair-trade items is another decision that, in and of itself, might have only a small impact per household. But for our church it has become a way of living today that is in sync with God's future for our world. Each small step, every tiny decision, functions as an act of faith helping us become the kind of people who naturally love our neighbors.

As a congregation we've learned that fair trade isn't really a luxury at all; it's not a cost we might choose to pay above and beyond the normative price set by the free market, as if we're choosing to go beyond this "actual price" out of generosity. No, fair trade is the *true* cost of the item or service. Cheaper free-market products are subsidized prices, the cost we're willing to pay while allowing a nameless, faceless "other" to subsidize our lifestyle through their own sweatshop, slave, or stolen labor.

In 2015, we as a church decided to buy fair-trade chocolate candies in bulk for our members to hand out on Halloween night. It has become impossible to unlearn the surprising but clear case about connections between Western interests and the slave trade abroad. We knew that the chocolate market employs enormous numbers of slaves worldwide and that candy companies like Nestlé remain part of that system. How unfortunate it would be to preach abolition while living a life that supports slavery.

One household's daily, small decision to be part of the solution and not the problem has cascaded into entire communities living a more just life for the sake of our global neighbors. We live in a small world, and the gospel helps us see how important those connections really are.

FOR BETTER OR FOR WORSE

Everything is interrelated. War, local economies, spiritual health, poverty, creation, chocolate. For better or for worse, we are citizens of this one world—our world, the created world, the only world we've got. Events on a global scale affect your neighbors next door, and choices you make ripple to the four corners of our globe.

When you step outside your door, what around you makes your world feel small? International corporations, military bases, climate change, friends with PTSD? How does the gospel bring a sense that the world is at your doorstep? As you think about these questions, you may find clarity on what neighbor care might look like for you and your faith community.

In the next chapter, we'll explore a third Christian practice that turns our perspective downside up. In doing so, this practice helps us see—and live in—the righted world God intends.

NINE

Read the Bible with Black Lives Matter

THERE'S A PHOTOGRAPH of a beautiful young woman whose innocent smile horrifies me. Through the grainy pixels, it's clear she has taken care with her appearance, as she likely always had. Perhaps she aimed for delicate fashion that appeared as if no special effort had been made. There are no hints of anxiety in her choice of flowered cotton dress on that hot August day in 1930, or in the relaxed way she holds her boyfriend's hand. I can imagine her giggling with her friends earlier in the day as they gossiped about the latest news. She looks like the girl next door, a girl I might have dated had I been born seventy years earlier.

The camera captures the crowd around her charged with the energy of thrill. It looks in all ways like a bonfire party held in a local boy's field. A huge oak tree stands tall behind them; it appears to be a normal spot where this crowd regularly gathers.

The scene looks normal in every way, except for two lynched black bodies hanging dead from a branch in the background. Strange fruit indeed, as Billie Holiday sang, swaying in the breeze. This is a crime scene and not a party.[1]

The lynching mob in this photograph had used sledge-hammers to break into the county jail. They then tortured and hung nineteen-year-old Abram Smith and eighteen-year-old Thomas Shipp as an act of deterrence. Thousands of white folks poured into Marion, Indiana, from across the state to witness the spectacle. Hundreds of black families poured out of town, fleeing to safety.

Ten years earlier Indiana Wesleyan University had been founded in Marion. Today it is one of the largest evangelical Christian universities in the country. I have no idea how or if students or faculty there participated in or protested this crime, but we know that at that time some American Christians supported Jim Crow, as they had slavery a century earlier. Others remained quiet in the face of such terror, and still others worked to dismantle oppression. I wonder what was said in chapel at Indiana Wesleyan that next day.

When I hear stories like this, I find myself automatically going into "Would I have . . . ?" mode. Would I have been at that party? Would I have tried to put a stop to it? Would I have used my pulpit to support or dismantle racism? It's humbling to think how difficult it would have been to be different from the majority in my community.

For many people of privilege, these are the two main characters we identify with: those who did and those who didn't support racial terrorism. But consider identifying with the third

---

1 Photograph taken by Lawrence Beitler on August 7, 1930, in Marion, Indiana. The image may be viewed at the website of America's Black Holocaust Museum, http://abhmuseum.org/wp-content/uploads/2012/01/7-Beitler-photo -best.jpg.

characters in the photograph: the dead men hanging from the tree. What if you weren't struggling to live faithfully but were merely struggling to live in a culture that hated you? What if you were part of a community that was terrorized through lynching mobs and bodies hung on trees?

Of course, for millions of oppressed peoples this isn't an exercise at all; it's just the way things are in cultures that promote death. When I imagine myself in this way, perhaps hidden behind locked doors after a buddy had just been lynched, it makes an incredible difference.

As well it should, because perspective matters. Consider, for instance, how you think about the ocean. Your mind may first go to beaches littered with seashells and sandcastles, the waves rolling in. If you're like me, this is the main way that you experience the ocean. Now think about how different the experience of the ocean is for a scuba diver, surrounded by an underwater world of life and color. To understand an ocean, it's pretty obvious we need both—or more—perspectives.

It's no different for our faith when our context or perspective changes. If I were part of a community shackled by fear and desperate for change, I would cling to hope. Faith from this side of the tree would be about deep trust, prayers of protection, and a call for liberation. There's no walking away or time out for people who are part of the lynched community; your doors will always be locked and your eyes habitually on the lookout.

On the other hand, the "Would I have . . . ?" mode leaves me feeling guilty and groveling on my knees for absolution. When the faith of the privileged and comfortable addresses sin management and morality with the promise of eternal life, it does little to change the reality of racial injustice.

Feeling guilty or angry about our part in the story of race is hardly the best motivator for loving or liberating communities of oppression. But according to the biblical narrative, our spiritual flourishing or famine is connected to our awareness of dependence on God. This is something that those in lynched communities of faith have already learned.

Let's press more deeply into the faith of the marginalized and how their unique perspective may clarify and correct understandings of what the common good or the shalom of God really is. In this practice, I invite you to intentionally value the voice of the poor and pushed-out in your community. Why? Because seeing the world through the eyes of God may happen when we see the world from where Jesus lived—on the margins.

WHO DECIDES THE COMMON GOOD?

Seeing the world from the perspective of the victimized and marginalized may very well change the way that we define the common good. Typically defined by those with power and privilege, abstract ideas like *common good* and *national interest* can be filled with any meaning desired, leaving these concepts void of any meaning when disconnected from the biblical notion of shalom. But letting marginal communities define the common good gives a clear and compelling definition to the Bible's biggest word.

Remember Brendan Reilly and the increased efficiency of Cook County Hospital's treatment of heart patients by simplifying the diagnostic process? A simple four-factor algorithm performed better than piles of information. I've come to believe that seeing the world from the perspective of vulnerable citizens is the Bible's simple algorithm that helps Christians diagnose our world accurately.

Over and over again, Scripture locates God as being *with* those on the margins—migrants, poor, sick, imprisoned. For Luke, both the poor and those *with* the poor receive the kingdom of God. Proverbs, Jeremiah, Matthew, and Hebrews all suggest that relationship with the poor is relationship with God himself. The early church leader James said it's the poor who have the healthiest faith.[2]

The triad "widows, orphans, and strangers" is used so often it's as if the biblical authors are offering us a coded automatic response. Our response to their needs can be simple, quick, without much need for tests or lengthy verification. You see— you do.

Jesus' ministry was not to gain unlimited power and popularity but to "bring good news to the poor" (Luke 4:18). Because of this, I wonder if we could ever understand the cross from the perspective of Rome. Or do we need to see it from where Jesus was—with the oppressed, the group of people who know what it feels like to have a body's skin stretched on hard wood?

In his book *The Cross and the Lynching Tree*, James Cone talks about the importance of experiencing Christianity from within the lynched community. He talks about how the black church has linked black victims with the crucified Christ, saying, "Until we can see the cross and the lynching tree together, until we can identify Christ with the 're-crucified' black body hanging from the lynching tree, there can be no genuine understanding of Christian identity in America, and no deliverance from the brutal legacy of slavery and white supremacy."[3]

For Cone, there is no better way to understand Christ than from the perspective of black victims. "The clearest image of the crucified Christ was the figure of an innocent black victim, dangling from a lynching tree."[4]

---

2 See Proverbs 19:17; Isaiah 58:6-11; Jeremiah 22:16; Matthew 25:31-46; Luke 6:20; 12:30-34; Hebrews 13:2; and James 1:9-11; 5:1-8.
3 James Cone, *The Cross and the Lynching Tree* (Maryknoll, NY: Orbis Books, 2011), xv.
4 Ibid., 93.

Jesus believed we will find our spiritual anchor where we find God: on the margins and in the lives of the poor and pushed-out. I'm not arguing here for what some call God's "preferential option for the poor" (though I believe that is theologically appropriate). I'm asking whether the poor have a preferential option for God. The marginalized have an important and meaningful role in clarifying our image of God. At the very least, those pushed to the margins have an alternative perspective, like our scuba diver below the water line. And multiple voices, multiple ways of reading the same text or city, can lead us to greater faith.

I'm tempted to leave it at that and ignore the warnings of Scripture that wealth and power will lead us astray. But my faith will suffer if I ignore that God wasn't merely *with* the Israelites in Egypt; he was also very much *against* Pharaoh. I cannot ignore the fact that the New Testament authors found it nearly impossible to interpret positively a story of someone with great means. Jesus did more in the wilderness than learn to hunger for God for forty days; he denied all opportunities to privilege. We've got to learn to trust the poor and pushed-out, to take them at their word. Not because they will always be right, but because we believe Jesus, the poorest and most pushed-out of them all.

But let's be honest: it's impossible to deny how consistently marginalized communities and individuals do get it right. Like the black church in the American South, the First Nations peoples of Canada, the Palestinian church under the thumb of racial oppression. Like Dietrich Bonhoeffer, Dorothy Day, Oscar Romero, and women during the suffragette movement. I would be misguiding you if I didn't take to heart how insistent the Bible is in locating God with the poor and pushed-out rather than the powerful.

RACISM 3.0

The gap between the above and below perspectives of reality is hardly more obvious than when we talk about race. Police brutality and the massive racial imbalance in our devastatingly high prison population are two of many topics that can polarize dominant culture citizens and marginal citizens. Pastor Hannah Bonner has felt this shake her core and rattle her faith in humanity.

In the summer of 2015, the Waller County sheriff publicly demanded of her, "Why don't you go back to the church of Satan that you run?" This was quite a shock, given that her supposed "satanic" offense was a commitment to prayer vigils for the black community. After the confusing and strange death of Sandra Bland while in police custody, Hannah visited the Waller County jail every day to pray and seek wisdom. To the black community, Hannah's public witness has been a profound celebration of black humanity.

But for Hannah, a fully credentialed white pastor of St. John's Church in downtown Houston, a traditionally black church, to be called "the church of Satan lady" reveals that she also acted to liberate a society still held captive by race. The sheriff has been one part of a larger system that has worked tirelessly to quiet the call of justice for Sandra Bland. Hannah has been followed, surveilled, yelled at, mocked, and threatened. Doors at the county courthouse were blocked, shade trees were cut down, long-postponed remodeling projects suddenly became a priority; all to limit access of the praying protestors.

America's original sin is rearing its spiritually impoverished head yet again. Racism has shown an incredible fluidity throughout our history. It seems to have nearly infinite capacity to morph into new expressions and practices. It has become increasingly effective to move beyond arguments about racism and begin to explore *racialization*. Racism defined as an individual act of animus can be easily dismissed, but it's impossible to ignore that race still works in unique and sometimes dangerous ways.

In the formative years of Houston, racialization led the Allen brothers, speculators from New York, to lay claim to land occupied for thousands of years by the native Karankawa people. By the Juneteenth celebration of emancipation thirty years later, 50 percent of Houston consisted of Africans forcibly and legally migrated.

Racialization adapted under Jim Crow segregation to take a new form: the suffocating lies of "separate but equal," cross burnings, Christian white supremacy, preachers espousing doctrines of segregation, whites-only establishments, and public lynchings. During the civil rights era, racialization morphed yet again, this time into white tactics of hostile blockade, pulpit silence, and subtle calls to "slow down."

What is common in each of these unique adaptations is that they each have a social component embedded in culture and practices, something out of any one individual's control. Equally common to these adaptations is awareness by the black community that social problems need social solutions.

The Black Lives Matter movement was birthed by three black women in response to the legal acquittal of the man who killed Trayvon Martin, an unarmed black teenager. I remember this acquittal all too well. In the days after the acquittal, several black pastor friends in Houston called to ask me if I planned to mention Trayvon Martin from the pulpit on Sunday. It was obvious they would and thus weren't calling for advice. What they needed to hear from me, an assumed white ally, is that the white church stood by them in solidarity. I know of no black churches in Houston that didn't mention the acquittal, and only a handful of white churches like mine that did.

But for Alicia Garza, Patrisse Cullors, and Opal Tometi, this was an opportunity to turn black patterns of oppression into an expression of black resilience. What started as a social media voice by two queer black women and a Nigerian immigrant has grown since August 2013 to become a powerful movement for social change. Trayvon, Michael Brown, Eric Garner, Tamir Rice are all names of black men victimized by racism's latest incarnation—a kind of modern-day lynching.

Alicia, Patrisse, and Opal stand in an awesome line of black women leaders including Ida B. Wells, Ella Baker, Diane Nash, and Fannie Lou Hamer who have driven social movements. And yet, like these women, they too have struggled with being marginalized within the movement because they are women. I believe this is why Hannah Bonner's mission to keep Sandra Bland's story in the minds of Christian brothers and sisters is so essential to spiritual health.

"Say her name" is a powerful reminder that black women are and have always been front and center in the movement of racial justice. For these women the insistence that black lives matter is not a negation of anyone else's life, but an insistence that celebrating black lives is essential for everyone's liberation from racialization—black and white alike.

Pastor Hannah's Black Lives Matter faith has opened her to take this more radical posture. This movement from below has helped Hannah identify more as a follower of a public way than as a keeper of a private God. The pushed-out aren't on the margins due to choice or poor life management. They have, as the nomenclature suggests, been pushed out by someone for some reason. This is a reality in which we all participate. The very public theology of Black Lives Matter also reveals that something other than the poor makes the poor *poor*. There are powers and cultural inertia beyond our control that continue to trip us up, a truth seen clearest from the bottom up, not top down.

So, too, is there faith and Spirit that is beyond our control that continues to empower Christian witness. The executed-now-risen God of the margins is with us in our witness.

SANDRA STILL SPEAKS

I've suggested that the faith of Jesus and other marginalized peoples may be unique. But how is this so? What can we learn from seeing the world from within the lynched community that we might easily miss when seeing the world through the lens of white guilt? How do marginal peoples cling to God and root themselves in Jesus in ways that may strengthen our public witness? What correctives and challenges might a Black Lives Matter faith give to the North American church?

Sandra Bland was a passionate Christian who once said, "My purpose is to . . . stop all social injustice in the South." At the center of her faith, and of the faith of many in Black Lives Matter, lives is a robust Jesus: a Christ who brings freedom, not escape. Sandra and others like her cling to the Jesus who boldly confronted religious and political leaders more than to the love-your-enemies Jesus who may so quickly be co-opted to silence voices of social change. From the time of slavery's abolition movement, the black Jesus has differed markedly from the Jesus of dominant culture. While white pastors preached repeatedly from Old Testament texts, abolitionists always rooted their gospel in the life and message of Jesus. Even secular leaders then (Frederick Douglass and W. E. B. DuBois) and now reference this radical element in Jesus.

During the time of the civil rights movement, the Jesus of Billy Graham was a sacrifice whose death came at the hands of an angry God, not a radical leader whose death came at the hands of an angry mob. Jesus was a ticket to a better place, not a moral model to create a better world.

In her powerful "Sandy Speaks" videos, filmed before her death in the summer of 2015, Sandra intentionally and repeatedly named her faith as the foundation of her hope for liberation and healing. This same foundation is also present for Hannah Bonner, whose soul is becoming unbound the more deeply she lives inside the faith of the black community.[5]

Less a problem to be legislated or tumor to be removed, racialization is a sickness in need of healing. Novelist Chimamanda Ngozi Adichie jests in her book *Americanah* that we all suffer mild, medium, or acute levels of what she calls "racial disorder syndrome."[6]

This is undoubtedly true for me. Not that I am or ever have been a blatant racist, and I doubt that you are either. But I have been racialized to think about everything, from missions to theology, through a white-default lens. And I have grown increasingly hopeful that if Jesus is truly the one who takes away the sins of the world, then the broken way that race works in Houston is on his list.

This is why I've spent the last few years as a member and participant engaged in a multiyear journey called Healing the Brokenness. In a series of intentional conversations and lectures, a group of us have learned that race continues to account for deeply ingrained patterns of privilege and inequality, especially in the areas of incarceration, gentrification, and criminal justice. But I've also learned the power of being liberated from the soul-twisting lies of racial superiority. Being part of a learning community such as this connects me to folks as we do the hard work of surgically separating ourselves from a broken story of race.

5 Read Hannah's public blog, *Soul Unbound*, at http://soulunbound.com/.
6 Chimamanda Ngozi Adichie, *Americanah* (New York: Anchor, 2014), 390.

I believe deeply that pursuit of shalom in our communities demands we prioritize marginal voices and that we learn from Christian voices like Sandra's, who still speaks to us today. Doing so reveals truths we may not arrive at any other way: how spiritually bankrupt white privilege can make us, how spiritually vibrant the faith of lynched and oppressed communities can be, and how Christian action becomes prophetic when we allow the poor and pushed-out to lead us. If all we have is one model, sooner or later we'll start to believe it. Whatever ways you find to see the world from the margins is fantastic. Here are several suggestions to get you started.

THE BIBLE FROM BELOW

A few local congregations have taken steps such as these to broaden their perspective.

Listen to the marginal voices that you already know. A turning point in my congregation's understanding about immigration came when we invited a sister church whose members were recent immigrants to come share stories of migration. Listening to their stories helped us see how similar our own ancestors' migration stories actually were. And it helped us to understand what good news might look like for their community today.

Read the Bible from below, where Jesus lived. Be intentional about exploring marginal texts and authors as you study Scripture. Put yourself in the life of a Christian victim of ISIS, a gay nephew forced out of the church, the homeless person you pass on the way to work, an irregular migrant in search of work, a coworker wracked with grief, a refugee from Syria, a black man who fears for his life when in the presence of police. Then ask yourself, "What is the good news of God for them? What is God doing in their lives? How is it the same and different from what God is doing in my life?"

Classic marginal hermeneutics, such as black liberation, Anabaptist, Latin American, liberation, *mujerista*, indigenous, queer, and many other theologies, can help us see through the eyes of the people Jesus spent the most time with.[7] In recommending these resources I'm not suggesting that these theologies are *better*; I'm suggesting that they are *different*. I have found that listening deeply to the voices of the marginalized has profoundly shaped my understanding of discipleship and the common good.

Write an autobiography of race. This type of autobiography helps explore what your place is in the story of race in America. An excellent resource for this is the book *From Churches, Cultures and Leadership.*[8] Understanding better who we are can be transformative in understanding the stories of others.

Map out where in your own community the marginalized live. Grab a local map and a handful of pushpins. Place a pin everywhere on your map you might find someone Jesus mentions in Matthew 25:31-46. Ask yourself where the poor neighborhoods are located. Where do the immigrants live? Where are the health clinics that serve the uninsured? Where are the prisons?

As a faith community, think about what it would look like for these communities to be restored to wholeness. What would have to change for these communities to function as designed? What is the gospel message for these people? What blocks might your community put up to them experiencing it?

One of the greatest gifts that urban ministry has given my family and me is the diversity of people and perspectives present here. Learning from these alternative voices has been one of

7 For more on these theologies, see the recommended reading list in the study guide at www.heraldpress.com/Studygds/.

8 Mark Lau Branson and Juan F. Martinez, *Churches, Cultures and Leadership: A Practical Theology of Congregations and Ethnicities* (Downers Grove, IL: InterVarsity Academic, 2011).

the most foundational ways I've come to understand and love how God is bringing shalom to my community.

Should this surprise us? Christians are people who have set their own stories aside to accept an invitation from someone who himself lived in the margins and shadows of empire. Certainly our own faith and faithfulness will be reshaped when we go where Jesus is and look at the world from his social location and not our own.

In our final section, we'll continue to look from the bottom up at how God is restoring all things. As we do so, we'll keep in mind how bottom-up hermeneutics helps to clarify the gospel, and thus triage life on our streets.

Part IV

The Gospel Gift of Restoring Justice

Until we fight for the rights of others as we would for our own there will be no justice.

—ANONYMOUS

TEN

Houston, We Have
a Problem

I N 1988 HABITAT FOR HUMANITY began to operate in Houston's Fifth Ward, a black neighborhood that earned the title in 1979 as "the most vicious quarter of Texas." The first home that Habitat built in this neighborhood was for a grandmother who cared for five of her grandchildren.

Stephen Fairfield was a successful young developer whose passion to integrate his faith and vocational skills led him to this endeavor. An outsider in the Fifth Ward, Stephen brought the best of his skills and passion to this neighborhood that Habitat believed could greatly benefit from quality low-income housing. Stephen acted as the project manager and connected volunteers from area churches to the project in the Fifth Ward.

Given its notoriety, the Fifth Ward was regularly the recipient of outside white charity and service projects. These "mission bombs" were short lived, often disconnected from real, felt needs, and were not based on relationships. Habitat was intent on changing that.

Several weeks into their first build, Habitat volunteers had framed the wall studs and installed windows and doors. A successful week completed, they headed home for the weekend. When they returned Monday morning, however, they discovered the lumber, windows, and brand-new doors were gone.

A neighbor pulled Stephen aside and said to him, "You need a fence and a dog in this neighborhood."

Having arranged for the fence and for a spirited watchdog, Stephen and his crew set back to work. Again they completed the wall joists and installation of windows and doors. This time, as they returned to the house on Monday morning to continue to build, they discovered that not only had the lumber, windows, and doors been removed, but the dog and fence as well.

Stephen was stumped. Here he was, putting his faith into practice by bringing something good into a neighborhood with needs. Why weren't the residents accepting of this obviously worthwhile mission? This time, the neighbor told Stephen something that would change the neighborhood forever. "You need to talk with Pastor Harvey Clemons," the neighbor said.

Clemons was the well-known and deeply influential pastor of what was once the South's largest African American congregation. When he spoke, things happened. Stephen approached Clemons, not knowing how a pastor could help but eager to complete the project. Clemons liked the vision of Habitat and was happy to help a good cause. But he was not satisfied with addressing the Fifth Ward's housing crisis. He told Stephen that Habitat could build scores of homes but that they might simply form the foundation of the ghetto for the next twenty years. What was needed, Clemons said, was a holistic approach to restoring the Fifth Ward.

Invisible to Stephen, word quickly spread that Clemons and the Pleasant Hill Baptist Church were now involved in the Habitat build. The house was finished ahead of schedule.

When Pastor Clemons began his ministry at Pleasant Hills, his neighborhood was filled with broken windows, absentee landlords, lack of local businesses, and food deserts. He felt that in a setting filled with crumbling social safety nets, the gospel fell on flat ears. If the gospel solved eternal concerns, could it not also address these basic life concerns? Pastor Clemons asked himself: How can I preach that Christ has power over all when our neighborhood looks like this? If Christ is all-powerful, he thought, certainly together we can address the roots of poverty and injustice.

Divine discontent with current reality sparked a new dream for the Fifth Ward. A comprehensive vision for community redevelopment was born, which rooted members deeply in the gospel's holistic vision for personal and public salvation.

WITH LIBERTY AND JUSTICE . . .

When I started my ministry after graduating from Wheaton College, I would have assumed "justice" in this story meant finding and punishing the thieves. But in the Fifth Ward, as in most neighborhoods, doing justice isn't like mystery detection in popular fiction, in which you find the bad guys and prosecute them to the full extent of the law. If we believe that justice is about righting personal wrongs, our action is likely to be to get rid of all the bad guys. But there's far more going on in this story, and far more to understanding God's gift of justice to our neighborhoods.

When justice is about all life and community flourishing, then brokenness is a great way to think deeply about what's gone wrong. When we define injustice as brokenness, doing justice is like stopping the zombie apocalypse before it starts.

End-of-the-world-as-we-know-it literature like *1984*, *The Hunger Games*, and *The Walking Dead* points to a profound disconnect between the way things are and the way the world should be. Dystopian literature addresses our shared social anxiety. Sociologist Peter Dendle calls this genre "a barometer of cultural anxiety . . . tracking a wide range of cultural, political, and economic anxieties of American society."[1] It's a "stylized reaction to cultural consciousness and particularly to social and political injustices."[2]

Dystopias—zombie, biblical, or otherwise—assume everything and everyone is connected. This is a powerful insight to begin with, because everybody, from Martin Luther King Jr. (who spoke of the "single garment of destiny"[3]) to quantum physicists and evolutionary biologists, speaks of our interconnectedness.

And when something is broken it affects everyone, for the breakdown is in the community itself. As King also said, "Injustice anywhere is a threat to justice everywhere."[4] And since we're all connected, it means we're all part of the problem, and can choose to be part of its solution. The Bible's word for this—for broken relationships and broken community—is *in*justice. In Greek, this is the exact same word as *un*righteousness.

What ailed the Fifth Ward wasn't merely personal sin but also layers of sinful injustice that handicapped human flourishing for everyone.

In both Scripture and the American Pledge of Allegiance, when we say "justice for all," we're speaking to a quality of

1 Peter Dendle, 'The Zombie as Barometer of Cultural Anxiety," in *Monsters and the Monstrous: Myths and Metaphors of Enduring Evil*, ed. Niall Scott (New York: Rodopi, 2007), 45.
2 Kyle Bishop, "Dead Man Still Walking: Explaining the Zombie Renaissance," *Journal of Popular Film and Television* 37, no. 1 (2009): 18.
3 Martin Luther King Jr. "Letter from Birmingham Jail" in *Why We Can't Wait* (Boston: Beacon Press, 2011), 87.
4 Ibid.

community, a way of being together. And it's this quality of community—what the Bible calls *justice and righteousness*—that God is working for where we live, work, and play. There can be no peace or shalom without justice, but wherever justice is found, there you will find shalom.

Would it surprise you to know this quality of community is such good news that Christian Scripture intertwines it with gospel? For many of us, gospel and justice no more belong together than mangoes and hot chili spice. The gospel is over here, pure and simple, giving salvation to the lost. And justice is dirty work of the secular world, a far lesser concern that hardly belongs in the same sentence.

I get this a lot from people: bafflement about this connection and confusion about what justice is. I always answer in the same way. Prophetic justice advocacy is tied to theology; it speaks to who God is and how God chooses to be in the world. The breadth and depth, height and length of God's love for the world is so all-encompassing that it passionately addresses both those who are *lost* and that which is *broken*. Isaiah says that God loves justice, and I can't help but think that's because of his steadfast love for people.

For too long I misunderstood righteousness as legalistic sin patrol, concerned strictly with individual piety. But justice is the quality of right relationships that are healthy, flourishing, life-giving, working as designed, committed in covenant and joy, with shared resources aplenty.

The change of perception would have saved me more than a few exacting sessions of personal confession late into my junior high nights. It may also have given me a more dynamic road map to navigate through our complex world.

What I also didn't understand until well into adulthood is that justice and righteousness are two translations of the same

Greek word. Our English translations of the Bible often render the Hebrew and Greek word as "righteousness," when "justice" is equally acceptable.

We might be tempted to think of them as two expressions of a similar idea, like ice and water, or grace and kindness. To a certain extent, it's helpful to say righteousness is the inner quality essential for right relationships, whereas justice refers to the outer shared qualities that make right community possible. The concept certainly holds both connotations, though it is perhaps more like two strands of a DNA double helix, giving form and direction to the singular reality of healthy relationships and community.

God's justice has the power of restoration in its bones. It holds the power to transform lives. Perhaps that's why Paul mingles justice, Jesus, and gospel so intimately, saying the gospel of Jesus reveals the justice of God (Romans 1:16-17). Elsewhere Paul says God's version of justice takes the shape of Jesus' faithful lifestyle. We never find the work of justice portrayed as the dirty work of secular vocation. Instead, it's always an act of faith. Justice, righteousness, right relationships, the healing of social brokenness, reconciliation: these are all Jesus' gospel preached to the world.

God's coming kingdom *is* the long-awaited, restorative, right-making justice of God. When justice and righteousness are present, human communities will flourish. When they are absent, folks may easily fall through the cracks into poverty or hide from violence in the shadows.

... FOR ALL

So what does justice look like in the Fifth Ward and in neighborhoods like yours? Who are the recipients of God's gift of justice? Is it directed at the thieves who stole from Habitat, or as a gift to the grandmother? Is it about punishment or about healing the roots of poverty?

Justice, when given by God, is directed to those in need. It's shared like a feast for the hungry, coming in an abundance of courses—economic, social, cultural, racial, environmental, gender, territorial, and resource-sharing justice. A prophet invites everyone who thirsts to "come to the waters; and you that have no money, come, buy and eat! Come, buy wine and milk without money and without price. Why do you spend your money for that which is not bread, and your labor for that which does not satisfy? Listen carefully to me, and eat what is good, and delight yourselves in rich food" (Isaiah 55:1-2).

It's a pure gift from God, no less than grace or lovingkindness, and it organizes the kind of shared spaces that organically lead to healthy relationships and human flourishing.

We see this in biblical economics, which are concerned not with consistent economic growth but consistent economic distribution. God's concern is not primarily with individuals getting ahead, but communities that understand current reality and that collaborate for the common good. Practices as simple as keeping the Sabbath hardwire provision and protection of the poor and vulnerable into the social structure itself.

Jesus is quick to announce and live good news for the poor, including famously inviting us to pray for debt relief when he teaches us about prayer in the Sermon on the Mount. And for those of us with plenty, we share our goods because Christ has shared his gifts with us.

How had people's power in the Fifth Ward deteriorated so painfully that they were left with no hope? Why did poverty strike *this* neighborhood and leave others alone? What relationships were severed such that households were left to fend for themselves?

REDEVELOPMENT IN THE NAME OF CHRIST

In the Fifth Ward, the fabric that weaves everything together had been torn. Everyone—or perhaps no one—was to blame for this disharmony and broken shalom.

Such layered social brokenness demanded a layered social response. For too long the Christian response in the Fifth Ward was spiritualized or isolated from other layers of injustice. Saving souls and building homes are certainly good projects in and of themselves. But one doesn't heal cancer with a Band-Aid. Neither can you restore the wholeness of communities by addressing symptoms (theft, for example) rather than root causes.

Author Michelle Alexander sharply calls the mass incarceration of minorities "the new Jim Crow."[5] Our criminal justice system is weighed down with punitive approaches to nonviolent drug offenders. Black and brown men are represented far more in our prisons than their population percentage nationwide would suggest.

The building supplies stolen from the Habitat work site in the Fifth Ward proved to be something of a divine down payment on what would eventually become the Fifth Ward Community Redevelopment Corporation. Those windows and doors have been multiplied exponentially over the last twenty-five years as the landscape and spirit of the neighborhood have been revitalized.

Partnerships with local charter schools, Rice University, Starbucks, and area health centers have added to the "resurrection" this once-feared neighborhood is experiencing. Likewise, partnerships with Houston's main religious leaders have allowed the Fifth Ward's expertise to be exported throughout the wider Houston community on various issues such as immigration,

5 Michelle Alexander, *The New Jim Crow: Mass Incarceration in the Age of Colorblindness* (New York: The New Press, 2012).

incarceration, and economic development. God is stopping injustice in its tracks by bringing redemption to physical, spiritual, economic, and relational lives.

This is not the story of a handful of people or organizations, and it's certainly not the story of several windows gone missing. Rather, it's the story of what can happen when the gospel of God sparks imagination in our local communities.

Oh, and the grandmother whose doors and windows were stolen? She went on to raise her children, grandchildren, and great-grandchildren in her home, all while getting her college degree. She lives in the house to this day and paid her mortgage off about five years ago.

BOOMTOWN USA

Marketers tell me I live in "Boomtown USA," one of the nation's fastest growing, job-creating, construction-building, diversifying, and youth-attracting cities. Everything—from housing and culture to energy and science to medicine and restaurants—is electric here right now. You can see it in the construction cranes and the lightning speed of residential builds.

If all you see of Houston is what we advertise, you might believe it's a magical place to live and work. Billboards, magazines, and interviews all proclaim Houston as the next great American city. Truly, it's hard to miss our stability and wealth and the comfort they provide. Progress is everywhere, and the cameras know how to find it. This is a great example of how modern cities talk about themselves.

But then there is another story: the story of invisible Houston.

This story is more difficult to see, but it's the lived reality of far too many black and brown Houstonians. And it's what the Fifth Ward Redevelopment Corporation is working to change.

It is no fluke that, geographically, many of Houston's poorest communities are also our minority communities. These are the communities left behind by the city and its citizens. Here are our food, opportunity, and education deserts, environmentally disastrous Superfund sites, neighborhoods in need of public housing, places lacking adequate public transportation, and areas where police brutality is normative.

God seems to have special concern for the strangers, immigrants, and refugees inside our borders. Nearly every significant story in the Bible is a story of migration and the movement of people. The whole of the first five books of the Bible, the painful story of exile and return, and Jesus' childhood and ministry are all set in the context of immigration.

Faithful followers are invited to imagine themselves as part of God's liberation: "You shall also love the stranger, for you were strangers in the land of Egypt" (Deuteronomy 10:19). Crossing borders and radical hospitality are integral to God's narrative, and therefore ours as well.

My mind turns to friends Noe, Guermo, Francisco, and others at the Living Hope Wheelchair Association, some of the most courageous and faithful Christians I know. They minister to the marginalized of the marginalized among us: undocumented immigrants with disabilities. Marginalized for not having papers, and marginalized again for their disabilities. Many of their members have been hurt on the job (often because of poor labor laws) and are regularly without healthcare coverage or large family systems of support.

These men and women do all they can to ensure that our city's most vulnerable members are cared for. These friends are precisely who Jesus had in mind in Matthew 25 both as the kind of people we should become (people who love the marginalized) and the kind of people whom God values (migrants, the poor, sick, imprisoned).

Recently a member told me that Living Hope has given him "a reason to live again, because I felt dead when this started. Now you are my family. I want to help those who have experienced what I have." Living Hope is a missional community offering so much more than needed medical supplies. They offer community, dignity, and the chance for people with spinal cord injuries to join God in ministry. They constantly change my mental model of what it means to be "fully human, fully alive," as well as the qualifications for mission.

FAITH AND JUSTICE

One community that often feels left out of our understanding of just economics is that of low-wage workers. We know that the gospel is good news for absolutely everyone. But it's good for no one if not first good for the poor, the unloved, and the brokenhearted. Up is down, down is up. The last will be first; those who are hungry and poor are the blessed ones of God.

A 2012 study estimates that $993 million is recovered in stolen wages from low-wage workers each year, more than three times the total property stolen in robberies. The study also estimates that the thirty million low-wage workers in the United States lose, on average, $50 billion in stolen wages annually.[6] Wage theft takes many forms; the most prevalent are unpaid tips or overtime, or simply weeks of work gone unpaid. Unknown to most good churchgoers, wage theft is a widespread American injustice that's not isolated to a few individuals but is in the nature of the system itself.

---

6 Brady Meixell and Ross Eisenbrey, *An Epidemic of Wage Theft Is Costing Workers Hundreds of Millions of Dollars a Year*, EPI Issue Brief no. 385 (Washington, DC: Economic Policy Institute, 2014), http://www.epi.org /publication/epidemic-wage-theft-costing-workers-hundreds/.

Oscar's story is all too familiar. I met Oscar as part of my ministry to victims of wage theft. Oscar worked hard as a construction worker for a local company. As construction workers, he and his fellow coworkers labor in some of the most dangerous conditions for all area employees. Texas has few laws regulating safety for construction workers, has no mandatory drink breaks, and is the only state without mandatory workers' compensation. Perhaps this is why we lead the nation in deaths among construction workers, witnessing a worker death every two and a half days.

So it might come as a shock to hear that after working several weeks in this job, Oscar's employer began demanding overtime work but refused to provide overtime pay. As time went on, Oscar's wages began to fall and finally dropped below minimum wage. Not paying overtime and paying less than minimum wage are two of the first ways that employers steal wages, along with misclassifying workers as independent contractors, or taking inappropriate deductions.

To this day Oscar is still owed $3,500, about half of what he earned. His employer has not shown up in court to give Oscar his due. Oscar, like other low-wage workers in his position, was forced to make a tough decision when his wages were stolen. Should he invest substantial time and money (that he'd earned but not received) in recovering his stolen wages? Or should he cut his losses and find another job? Oscar chose to advocate for what he and others have earned.

Perhaps you assume in a story like this that some nebulous "authority" would quickly clean this mess up. Not so in Texas. Texas's rules and ordinances almost all favor business over people; when the system is designed to uphold the status quo, it is hard to "win" a case.

Oscar, as have many, had to stand up himself to address this crime. He also chose to stand with others to restore an entire system that was broken. His faith propelled him to seek more than just what was owed him individually and to push for fair and legal pay for all workers.

The missional community at the Fe y Justicia (Faith and Justice) Worker Center works against tremendous odds to recover stolen wages for low-wage workers. They minister to victims of wage theft through advocacy and community building. They do this because they understand there is a problem, and because no one else in the city has an eye for this community.

When employers are evasive or ignore the center's efforts to recover stolen wages, our faith-leaders team steps into action. We travel with the employee to the business office to confront owners about their wage theft and work with them to make amends. Often employers will deny the stories, no matter how much documentation you can provide. But our center has recovered thousands of dollars for families that need the income. I've stood in solidarity with dozens of low-wage workers like Oscar as they sought the pay that was stolen from them by employers. Over the years I've seen countless times how effective the voice of the faith community can be in wage-theft ministry.

I know these small acts of ministry can't change an entire city's economy, but we do what small acts we can. Whether we succeed in recovering money or not, I'm always aware that the action itself has formed me to become the kind of person who cares about justice.

I'll never forget an impromptu Bible study with a corporate executive in his high-rise office. A 2010 campaign we called Justice for Janitors was in full swing, seeking safer working conditions and living wages for the janitors who cleaned Houston's largest office buildings. David Atwood and I were part of a faith-leaders team who, over the course of several weeks, met with about a dozen building owners and tenants.

In one of our meetings, we shared how we felt Christianity was a call to ensure that every worker had what they needed to live well. We had made this same presentation to others and had been run out of the door or politely ignored. But in this meeting, our host pulled out a Bible and asked us to look together at God's wishes for a just economy.

I've been surprised by how often Christian business leaders resist their role in wider systems they are a part of. Too many are unaware of the actual power they have for change, and too many keep ethics and faith separate. But not all do, and increasingly you'll find business leaders taking responsibility to do what they can. Our efforts in this 2010 campaign, and again in 2013, secured higher wages and safer working conditions for the janitors in Houston.

JUST OUTSIDE YOUR DOOR

The two stories of Houston remind me of a parable Jesus told about a twice-blind man. In it he tells the story of a wealthy man unable to see a poor man who lingers daily right outside his door. Maybe it's because he was trained to see the wrong things. Jesus seems to say as much: "Your ambition is to look good in front of other people, not God. But God sees through to your hearts. He values things differently from you. The goals you and your peers are reaching for God detests" (Luke 16:15 The Voice).

But Jesus knows the wealthy man to be twice blind. Not only is he unwilling to see the poor man, but he's also unable to see what's spiritually right in front of him. He already had "the law of Moses and the writings of the prophets," and yet he was blind to the loving lifestyle they called him to live. Clearly defined action should have been for him—and can be for us—the direct outgrowth of clear biblical interpretation.

Who do you see when you step outside your front door? Is there anyone there you've been blind to? Is there anything in God's Word you've been blind to?

You may find people who need affordable housing, the marginalized of the marginalized desperate for healthcare, or workers whose wages have been stolen. Perhaps even entire neighborhoods are struggling under the weight of various giants of injustice.

I bet somewhere beyond your doorstep you'll also find churches and nonprofits filled with people who are seeking justice and quality of life for others. Most of our cities already witness to a more powerful story than the story of injustice or crime. They are witness to the kinds of things God does when love hits the streets through ordinary people just like you.

What do you see God already doing in your community? How are you being called to join?

ELEVEN

Congratulations, You've Been Called!

WHEN LINDA WHITE'S anger boiled over, she was ready to kill someone. She certainly wanted to, and most Texans would have supported her.

Gary Brown and Marion Berry had recently escaped from Houston's Casa Phoenix rehab center for youth and met Linda's daughter Cathy O'Daniel at an area gas station. After kidnapping and raping her, Berry pointed a gun in her face.

Cathy O'Daniel's last words would, years later, liberate White from her hate. "I forgive you. And God will too," Cathy told her killers.

But hearing those words was years away for Linda.

The two boys were juveniles and ineligible for the Texas death penalty, so White advocated lowering the legal execution age to thirteen. This wasn't the crazed voice of an angry parent. The groups and messages that surrounded her were never about healing, but hate, and getting even.

She saw the same hate in the faces of her students at Sam Houston University when they discussed what they wanted to do to a mother who recently drowned her two children. Over time, however, Linda and her husband, John, found they just didn't have enough energy to go on hating so deeply.

Something would need to change. Something more than forgiveness and different from punishment needed to happen. What she needed was to make things right—to find healing and a sense of purpose now that her life had been violently interrupted.

There was only one place she could find that, and only one man who could give it. Marion—her daughter's killer—had continued his violent behavior in prison and was unable to meet her. But Gary's behavior was markedly different. He showed contrition, and he was hungry to make things right.

Together with a mediator and Cathy O'Daniel's daughter, Ami, Linda eventually found herself face-to-face with her daughter's killer in his prison's chapel. During the next hours they talked about the impact the murder had had on their lives. Linda was liberal in sharing the bad and the good of the previous years. Her granddaughter Ami spoke freely to Gary about the pain of growing up without a mom.

Their conversation put the White family back in control, and allowed Gary to describe the details of the crime and its devastating impact on his own life. This is how Linda heard her daughter's powerful last words: "I forgive you. And God will too."

In all the misguided promises of closure her tough-on-crime community offered, Linda had found nothing that brought healing. But hearing how her daughter had remained true to herself and her faith to her last breath did. Since then Linda has stayed in limited contact with Gary, even helping him get his birth certificate when she heard he was having trouble finding work or getting a driver's license after his release from prison. (Gary became eligible for early release in 2010 under a new law to alleviate prison overcrowding.) Linda has become an amazing evangelist for healing practices for the victims of crime, and she travels extensively to promote restorative justice in prisons and schools.

The pain of Linda's loss has always been with her. But so too has the feeling that things had been made right and that God's gift of restorative justice had made the world just a little bit better.

MEAN PEOPLE DON'T SUCK

People getting what they need as the basis of divine justice? This would be enough, wouldn't it? It would be amazing to know that God makes it rain on the just and the unjust for the sake of the common good.

But what about the actual people involved? What does justice look like when we zero in on the very real story of a victim and her offender? If justice is able to change a community's reality before crime, does it also offer good news *after* it's occurred? Specifically, what do you do with the free riders who steal, bully, or kill their way to the top? In other words, what do we do with the mean people?

From the zero-tolerance policies of schools to our crowded, private, for-profit prisons, we have operated under the assumption that punishment is effective. We're led to believe mean people suck and need to be neutralized, which is why we're eager to elect officials who are "tough on crime."

This traditional mental model of justice is often referred to as *retributive* or *punitive justice*. Colloquially, "an eye for an eye and a tooth for a tooth" captures this mind set well, as do cultural phrases like law and order, crime and punishment, and people getting what they deserve. Traditional forms of justice focus on establishing individual blame for crimes against the state.

When guilt is assured, "justice" inflicts punishment that is perceived to fit the crime or harm done. Criminal reform is sidelined in an effort to divide and protect the innocent from the guilty, all in a strong defense of the status quo. The main parties are the offender and the authorities (such as the state or a school), with little focus on the needs of the victims.

I see this in the Roman god Zeus, who sits on his heavenly thrown to zap people perceived as deserving punishment. And I see this from Hollywood all the time. But let's be honest: Do we ever see this in Jesus' life or teachings? Does he live a tit-for-tat life? Our answer matters, right? It matters because if we don't get Jesus right, we'll never get our mission right. It's kind of essential to understanding the Christian narrative that "we were in the heat of combat with God when His Son reconciled us by laying down His life" (Romans 5:10 The Voice).

Instead of returning hate for hate, Jesus teaches returning good for evil. He is often caught bringing folks who have broken relationships back into full standing with their people. Women, deemed second-class on multiple levels, are repeatedly given full restoration into the community and relationship with God. Jesus' own mother, the woman at the well, Mary Magdalene, the woman caught in adultery: all had been pushed out of the community but are then brought back by Jesus. So too are men with premeditated habitual sins. Insiders such as hated tax collectors Matthew and Zacchaeus, the armed revolutionary Simon the Zealot, Thomas who doubted, and Peter who broke his relationship in three devastating lies—all are restored to full relationship. And outsiders are reconciled as well. Saul planned to execute Christians but is transformed into their boldest mouth-piece. Jesus is not interested in the blame game; he wants both victims and offenders restored to full community.

Jesus imagines humanity as a peaceable community and calls his followers to be makers of peace rather than judgment and discord. He also gives us specific instructions on how to pull it off. Whether we are offender or victim, Jesus imagines us as initiators of community restoration, and promises us that when two or three are gathered to address conflict, he'll be right there with us (Matthew 5:23-24; 18:15-17). Reconciliation with each other is as central to salvation as is reconciliation to God.

In recent years, Christians and non-Christians alike have translated these biblical truths into a striking vision and prac-tice of criminal justice. Mimicking God's justice, the practice of restorative justice addresses the needs of victims and works to restore all involved to full community. Restorative justice is not just an idea but a movement that celebrates how central reconciliation is to faith. The movement focuses on the needs of victims, offenders, and communities, and works to repair in-jury and promote healing. Rather than asking "What does the offender deserve?" a restorative justice approach asks, "What can be done to make things right?"[1]

Restorative justice focuses our attention in an entirely differ-ent direction than does retributive justice. Instead of neutral-izing or punishing mean people, it works to discern what can be done to make things right again. This practice of conflict transformation focuses on discovering the harm done to ac-tual people, relationships, and the social fabric of communities. Victims have safe space to share openly about the impact of the offender's behavior. There's no script for this or expectation of forgiveness, and victims are in control of their own response.

---

1 Howard Zehr, *Changing Lenses: Restorative Justice for Our Times*, 25th anniv. ed. (Harrisonburg: Herald Press, 2015), 188.

Offenders, too, have space to share their own needs and contextual reasons for their behavior. When needs are identified, all parties involved can cooperate in searching for a solution, such as reparation, reconciliation, or otherwise healing what was broken. Since the main parties involved are not abstract systems but actual people, restorative justice is continually seeking personal and social transformation. In keeping offenders as full community members, the process guards against recidivism.

Traditional forms of punitive justice give bad people the punishment we perceive they deserve. Restorative justice gives all people involved what they actually *need*. At the heart of restorative justice is reconciliation of God, offenders, victims, and communities.

For God, mean people don't suck. They're humans in need of restoration.

DO WE DARE BELIEVE JESUS?

Such a significant shift in mental models reminds me a lot of science, which from time to time necessarily changes our mind-set and beliefs. Scientists Galileo, Darwin, and Einstein all pushed beyond common-sense models and courageously imagined new realities that were right in front of us all along. Astronomy, biology, and physics all took exponential leaps because scientists in these fields dared to see differently.

All this demands a pointed question: Do we believe Jesus? If you're reading this book, the likelihood is high that you believe *in* Jesus. But do we actually take him at his word? Do we believe that Jesus meant what he said and was talking to us? Hindu leader Mahatma Gandhi famously quipped, "I like your Christ; I do not like your Christians. Your Christians are so unlike your Christ."

Was Jesus right in reconciling with Peter, let alone in putting him in charge of future operations? Should he really have ignored acceptable law and let an adulterous woman off without even a slap on the wrist? And why in the world did he forgive the offenders who killed him when he was innocent of all charges?

Scattered throughout cities like Houston are communities of people daring to believe Jesus and take him at his word.

Schools in Houston and across the country are increasingly embracing this new model of addressing behavior. Zero-tolerance policies resulting in suspensions, expulsions, and incarcerating students all lead to greater rates of recidivism and to more dropouts. Giving students a chance to learn about the impact of their behavior and providing multiple avenues for full return to community are leading to increased educational opportunities and a decrease in the school-to-prison pipeline.

Randy Beeler is principal at a charter school a mile from my house. From top to bottom, this school is designed to implement and teach restorative justice as a life standard. Natalia Fernandez and dozens of others are doing the same throughout the school system in my community. These are programs with measurable results, offering skills that influence students throughout their lives. Student courts, circles of reconciliation, and victim-offender mediation are skills being lived and taught in these schools.

But this movement is not just flowing into our schools. In what is to me an almost inconceivable act of faith, restorative justice has been practiced not only in cases of nonviolent crime (such as vandalism and theft) but also in violent crimes, including murder. Scores of Houstonians like John Sage have mimicked the choices of Jesus in forgiving killers.

After the murder of his sister, John grew increasingly skeptical of our criminal justice system. His, his family's, and his community's needs were never addressed during the process of his sister's killer being tried and sentenced to death in the nation's busiest execution chamber. A guilty verdict did little to meet his actual needs.

Through prayer and much soul searching, John found healing in his faith and forgiveness. In 1998 he formed Bridges to Life to create space for a healing journey for victims. He's also committed to the painful work of ministering to offenders, to, as he says, "show them the transforming power of God's love and forgiveness."

Bridges to Life has brought more than twenty-three thousand offenders in fifty Texas prisons to willingly sit face-to-face with their victims or surrogate victims of similar crimes. Such meetings are carefully led with restorative practices that allow participants to share their own story and pain. Mimicking Jesus, John believes that mean people, their victims, and our communities all benefit when justice is restorative rather than retributive.

Schools, communities, churches, and prisons are all embracing the value and effectiveness of restorative justice. Bridges to Life has offices scattered throughout Texas and beyond. Yet certainly we've much more work to do.

What might justice look like in your community or congregation? How would your office or residence be transformed if practices of restorative justice were introduced?

SLAVES OF JUSTICE

I wonder how it happened for you.

Maybe your date begged you to see *Selma* and you couldn't stop praying that you'd have been on the right side of that bridge.[2] Maybe you were blindsided by news of modern-day slavery and human trafficking right where you live. Maybe your nanny, gardener, or office janitor has no papers, and you'd hate to see her separated from her children.

2 *Selma* is a 2014 Hollywood movie that tells the story of the voting rights campaign in Selma, Alabama, in 1964.

Maybe you were reading Scripture late at night or drinking beer with a friend and wondering if this is all faith is cracked up to be. Maybe you dared dream with Martin Luther King Jr., or you chuckled to hear how effective a group of Filipino wives were in stopping violence by the use of a "sex strike."

And then it happened.

You heard the voice whisper in your ear: *You were made for something bigger than yourself.* And you became interested—at least enough to read this book—in following the rabbit trail of justice wherever it leads. The door flew open and you walked in, bug-eyed as on your first day of work. People look at you funny and wonder if you're judging them with your newfound faith. Justice isn't, after all, casual. It's more like choosing the red pill and kissing ordinary goodbye. No matter how it happened, you are here: ready to do some justice, love a little kindness, and walk perhaps not all *that* humbly with God.

Following Jesus is like changing the entire script we live by, swapping it for the story of Jesus' liberating gospel.

But in this story, God is not keen on finger-snapping miracles or waving a magic fix-it wand. Billboards, sermons, tweets, and podcasts can barely begin to hold the entire depth and breadth of the gospel of God.

Instead of miracles and messages, God shows up in an even more surprising way: us. *We* are the evangelists invited to stoke the hope that God's restoring justice can come to *Houston as it is in heaven.*

Howard Thurman said it like this: "Don't ask yourself what the world needs. Ask yourself what makes you come alive and then go do that. Because what the world needs is people who have come alive."[3]

---

3 Quoted in Gil Bailie, *Violence Unveiled: Humanity at the Crossroads* (New York: Crossroad, 1996), xv.

Maybe when you think of people doing justice you picture nonviolent black marchers attacked by white bigots and their firehoses and dogs. Maybe you imagine union picketers on strike, angry crowds blocking traffic to your favorite retail therapy center, or Machine Gun Preacher fighting his way to justice in an Africa corrupted by slavery.[4]

When I think of people doing justice, I think of my good friend Jerry Wald. Together we affectionately call ourselves "justice nerds," which is pretty much who we are: a couple of ordinary guys trying to do what we can. And I think of a retired teacher named Judy Hoffhien; retired oil executive David Atwood; our city's coolest nun, Sister Ceil; and a bunch of moms you probably sit in front of at church. We're ordinary folks, one and all, who have a clear and compelling vision of the gap between what is and what should be, and a commitment to bridge that gap with new skills.

Doing justice well is an invitation to become a lifetime student of your city and to practice new skills as a community. New skills, powered by a new theological narrative, may catalyze churches to expend their best energies loving their neighbors and actively working for common-good justice where we live, work, and play.

STRENGTH FOR THE JOURNEY

Before I proposed to my wife, I broke up with her. No matter how much I *wanted* to love Hannah, no matter how many times I *chose* to love her, my heart wasn't able. I felt stopped, blocked from doing the very thing I longed for. Not until I paused and bravely dealt with pain that broke my heart as an abused child was I free to love and be loved. I learned that

---

4 *Machine Gun Preacher* is a 2011 Hollywood film starring Gerard Butler, and also a nonprofit organization (http://www.machinegunpreacher.org/).

shame is one of the hardest prisons to escape and that I needed someone else to break me out.

It's no wonder "O come, O come, Emmanuel, and ransom *captive* Israel" has long been my favorite Christmas lyric.

I didn't learn to love Hannah well because I wanted to (I already did). I learned to love by understanding my chains and letting God break them down the way water dissolves rock.

God can see our inner chains just as easily as those that entangle young women caught in human trafficking or low-wage workers without food or rent. Chains are chains, and God has the power to liberate us from what binds our souls and holds our world captive. Oppression and shame, unjust burdens and spiritual blocks, hawkish lies and hiding of our true selves: none of these are any match for our God.

Paul says if we're converted and have the Spirit of Christ in us, we'll be "free to serve *a different master, God's redeeming* justice" (Romans 6:18 The Voice). In Christ we're free from chains, and bound to eternal love. Jesus says we're blessed if we hunger for justice and blessed if we're persecuted for working for it. He says we need more of it than the religious elites have, and more of it than anything else we seek.

Jim Martin sees this in countless churches through the ministry of the International Justice Mission. Ordinary churches like yours and mine have accepted Christ's call to enter the dark world of violent modern-day slavery. And they've done this not as a social service or political stance but because of their deep commitment to a God of liberation.

International Justice Mission has witnessed victims and offenders freed from the terrible oppression of slavery, but also North American Christians freed from the constraints of traditional ideas about Christianity. Martin says, "There is a palpable and growing sense that the church, as envisioned and inaugurated by Jesus, is hardwired to take on the epic battles of good and evil in our world and that as we say yes to Jesus and enter this struggle, *we find life.*"[5]

Remember the classic Dr. Seuss book *Green Eggs and Ham*, in which the guy finally decides, after much cajoling, that he wants to eat green eggs and ham pretty much any and everywhere? Daily discipleship is kind of like that: doing justice on a boat or with a goat, in the rain or on the train, in the court or in the classroom, at work or with a jerk. I'll do justice here and there; I will do it anywhere!

But never alone, and never through our own strength. Justice work is as much about spirituality and belief as it is about morality and action. It's the natural lifestyle of those who have experienced freedom from inner chains and have given themselves to breaking the outer chains that oppress. I love the promise with which Jesus concludes his Sermon on the Mount: that our lives become unshakable when we do the things Jesus asked us to do (Matthew 7:24-25).

In the final chapter we look at a fourth Christian practice that helps transform us into slaves of justice. As we worship, the Spirit of the risen Christ may transform us to become the kind of people we were created to be: Christians who live justly, love kindness, and walk with our true God in humility.

---

5 Jim Martin, *The Just Church* (Carol Stream, IL: Tyndale House Publishers, 2012), 211–12.

TWELVE

Worship the God of Mission

YOU HAVE TO watch yourself with worship. It has a funny way of obliterating "normal."

When Harbor Church, which meets in one of Houston's religiously antagonistic neighborhoods, decided to explore the gospel of God's justice, they had no idea how transformative it would be. As they studied an ancient text from the prophet Isaiah, they were pushed to ask if they really did value the same people and things that God values. And if they did, were they actually living it out? Or was there a gap between what they believed and how they behaved?

Isaiah's word about spiritual practice proved to read and analyze Harbor Church folks far more than they read or analyzed it.

> This is the kind of fast day I'm after:
>   to break the chains of injustice,
>   get rid of exploitation in the workplace,

> free the oppressed,
> cancel debts.
> What I'm interested in seeing you do is:
> sharing your food with the hungry,
> inviting the homeless poor into your homes,
> putting clothes on the shivering ill-clad,
> being available to your own families.
> Do this and the lights will turn on,
> and your lives will turn around at once.
> (Isaiah 58:6-8 *The Message*)

This was not the well-behaved church topic they were used to engaging. This was more like a child you are asked to adopt who changes your life forever. And change them it did, as their capacity to embrace God's kingdom and all people grew with every trial-and-error act of hospitality. Weeks of worshiping the God who cares about the hungry, homeless, and naked oriented them to do the same.

What struck Betty and Jim Herrington was the unusual phrase "inviting the homeless poor into your homes." Surely this isn't something to take *literally*, is it? Surely the best way to minister to the homeless is through a local nonprofit, right? Regardless of how many blocks their mental models about discipleship could throw up, the Herringtons agreed that if needed, they would offer hospitality to the homeless poor.

It wasn't but one day later that their opportunity came to them, when they met Carlene and Bo, who were stuck in Houston without resources. Betty and Jim took them into their home, fed them, washed their clothes, and even had a mechanic friend donate $465 worth of parts and labor to get their car going again. The night they left the Herringtons' home, Bo and Carlene were caught with a crack pipe, had aided others in an unfortunate robbery, and had ungraciously slipped out the back door.

Both Harbor Church and the Herringtons were furious, and some members openly said it had all been a crazy mistake that should never have happened. Carlene and Bo were looked down on and treated harshly by this community. And then Betty spoke quietly into the contempt. "I don't think God sent them to us so we could help them," she said. "I think he sent them to us for us. They were here for twenty-four short hours. In a very brief time, God used them to reveal how much fear and greed there was in me. We have been an angry, selfish, judgmental community since they left. I think God used them to reveal what is in us."

Together, the Herringtons and their congregation have learned that until we treat people as Jesus treated us—rather than how *people* treat us—embracing God's restoring justice very much remains empty words.

The Herringtons' passion is not unique. They simply wanted to find out what God was doing and join in.

VALUING THE THINGS OF GOD

The English word *worship* simply means "worth-ship." When we praise God, we're ascribing worth to who God is in our lives and world. Worship is our way of saying that we affirm God's action and presence, and we value them enough to back them with financial and spiritual capital.

If we worship the God of love, we're valuing love as the fundamental principle of creation and training ourselves to love likewise. If we worship the God who rescues the oppressed and cares for the poor, we're forming ourselves to do likewise. If we believe in the God of exodus and resurrection, we work for similar liberation in the lives of those we love.

When we worship we're reminding ourselves how marvelously theological justice actually is. It's not an elective or secondary concern added after soul saving and evangelism have been accomplished. The New Testament authors celebrate justice by relating it to God, gospel, kingdom, divine goodness, shalom, salvation, liberation, and new creation.[1] You get the idea: it's a long list. This is what worship forms us to value.

Worshiping in community is like taking a vote to remind ourselves we're in this together. "All in favor say aye. All opposed?" That's right, God: my love for you is strong enough that at this time and with these people I'm pledging my sole allegiance to you. Can you think of a better metaphor than allegiance to describe what it means to love God with all your heart, soul, mind, and strength?

But keep this in mind. The God of justice isn't waiting for you to change the world. God is waiting for you to worship God. The rest will take care of itself.

The good news about injustice helps us to sort new events and experiences as if doing medical triage and to better understand the world we live in. Remember how Jesus said, "Very truly, I tell you, the Son can do nothing on his own, but only what he sees the Father doing; for whatever the Father does, the Son does likewise" (John 5:19-20)?

Perhaps I've repeatedly missed this plain text because for nearly my entire life, I've not connected the gospel to *God's acts*. I've been so locked into the ideas that God *loves me* and is interested in soul work, salvation, and sin management that I've assumed that's the answer to the question, "What does God do in our world?"

---

1 God: Psalm 146:7-9; Isaiah 61:8; Romans 3:26; gospel: Romans 1:16-17; 3:21-26; kingdom: Psalm 72; Isaiah 9:7; Matthew 6:33; Romans 14:17; goodness: Psalm 145:7; shalom: Psalm 72:7; 85:10; Isaiah 32:17; 52:7; Romans 5:1; salvation: Psalm 71:15; 85:8-11; Isaiah 51:4-6; 60:17-18; 61:10; Luke 1:68-79; liberation and new creation: Isaiah 65:17-25; 2 Corinthians 5:17-21; 2 Peter 3:13.

But if gospel is God's love for the *world*, it goes beyond what God is doing in me.

What, for instance, did justice look like at Selma's Edmond Pettus Bridge in 1965 on Bloody Sunday? Or what about the numerous stories of police brutality and violence against unarmed black men and boys in the United States? Who, we'd be right to ask, are the people most in need in the perceived culture war with our lesbian and gay friends and family? And when it comes to the war on terror, what creates the conditions in which terrorism is perceived as the most effective way to bring change?

Worship moves even one step further and orients us to live in the world as God is in the world.

FOLLOW THE LEADER

Prophets old and new creatively tie worship and justice intimately together. And the relevance flows both ways. Our worship is worth-*less* if our lives are not producing justice where we work and volunteer. And our missional, just living is crippled without vibrant God-centered worship.

In other words, worship clarifies our theology (who and how God is), invites us to value God and what God values, and forms us to imitate God. Isaiah invites us to come to God "that he may teach us his ways and that we may walk in his paths" (Isaiah 2:3). Prolific New Testament author John says we're able to love—to be the same way that Christ is in the world— "because he first loved us" (1 John 4:19).

If God loves the world, would the people you work alongside say the same about you? Might they say, "I'm not a person of faith, but man, does she ever love people." Or maybe they'd quip, "I'm heading to Hawaii for spring break. I can't believe you're giving up your vacation to build a Habitat home for someone across town!"

Notice how this-worldly God's concern is. God loves the world—*this* world—with its streets, buildings, businesses, and stuff of life. Worship can be so powerful and even dangerous because it agitates our spirits and creates divine discontent with the way things are. How could it not, if it connects us to the good news that God is re-creating a beautiful new world in our midst?

Not that any of that is normal for us. Sometimes we have to talk ourselves into valuing the people and things God values. Like the psalmist who needs a little personal pep talk before he can authentically ascribe worth to who and how God is: "Bless the Lord, O my soul, and all that is within me, bless his holy name. Bless the Lord, O my soul" (Psalm 103:1-2).

And many times words just aren't going to get us there.

I don't think it was a mistake that Jesus invited us to a meal instead of a sermon to remember his story. First he lays out the work order for our behavior, and then he shows us how to do it. "I give you a new commandment, that you love one another. Just as I have loved you, you also should love one an-other" (John 13:34).

And before you can even ask what that means, Jesus has broken a bread loaf and poured wine to share. The acts of breaking and pouring become symbolic performances of the self-sacrificial love we're called to give to the world. His radical hospitality toward betrayers and deserters is just one real-time example of what this means in daily life.

And sometimes, when reason and strength are exhausted, we need the church to awaken our imagination. Jesus modeled this in his bold prayer for God's kingdom to come "on earth as it is in heaven." Jesus' kingdom is Paul's "new creation." And before either it was Isaiah's vision of a "new thing" of flourish-ing life, filled with justice and friendships that sound downright miraculous.

How is your worship shaping you for mission? Is there such a thing as "missional worship"?

A MISSIONAL LITURGY

When church is viewed as being a purveyor of religious goods, as it often is in the West, then worship and spirituality can be twisted to mean the psychological soothing of our minds, the release of tension about how messed up our world is. It's a spirituality of adjustment, which of necessity takes the form of blessing empire, baptizing capitalism, and embracing info-tainment. If this is what worship is, then when we think about worship and mission together we may easily slip into thinking that our worship services are themselves to be attractive to out-siders. Services that attract people by their quality are likely not missional worship.

But the missional church isn't organized with pew-sitters in mind, and neither is its worship. Missional worship isn't some-thing we do for outsiders; it's what we do to become the kind of people who naturally follow Jesus right where we are. Missional worship creates space to encounter who and how God is in this world, appropriately shaping our belief, which in turn shapes our behavior.

Every aspect of a worship service can be deeply missional and form just disciples capable of making peace in our world. Songs; times of commitment; rituals of response, confession, lament, sending, and commissioning; eucharist; footwashing; and even financial giving can form disciples of Jesus. But the backbone of missional worship, its very heartbeat and passion, is praising who and how God is in our world.

Missional worship helps you see and mimic the God who is on mission to redeem where you live, work, and play. We gather together as practice for when we are scattered throughout our city. Worshiping together equips us for radical discipleship in the ordinary times of life.

In my congregation we do this intentionally throughout each of our worship services in four main movements.

Movement 1: Gathering. Worship's first movement is gathering as the church. As God's light in the world, we come together to cultivate a "we-consciousness" that draws us out of our habits of individualism. Gathering reminds us we are first members of the body of Christ, which together seeks to demonstrate God's alternative kingdom to the watching world.

Movement 2: Praise. The second movement of worship—valuing God through praise—can take many forms. Here we orient ourselves to who and how God is. Praising the God who was revealed most clearly in the incarnation of Jesus has everything to do with how well we love our neighbors and neighborhoods. Good theology is what makes your average worship hymnal one of the most powerful tools for justice.

Movement 3: Response. The movement of response is the invitation to join God's mission with our whole selves and commit to living the life Jesus has modeled for us to live. It's providing a conscience choice to align (or realign) ourselves with God and God's mission in the world, pledging allegiance to the kingdom of God rather than the kingdoms and culture of this world. As we've said, we're present with Christ in worship, to be present with our neighbors in life.

At the heart of Christian worship is the celebration of communion, sometimes known as eucharist. The ritual of the table reminds us powerfully how Jesus makes peace, and how we're invited to bring peace to our souls and streets. The pattern of breaking and pouring ourselves for the world is spiritually energized when we remember that the executed-now-risen Jesus is present with us today.

Movement 4: Commissioning. Our final movement in worship tells and celebrates that our God is on mission, seeking the holistic peace of Houston. It empowers us to become the sent ones of God who are specially tasked for special ministry in a special location: Houston.

THIS I BELIEVE

Can you see it with me? God who is "at work within us is able to accomplish abundantly far more than all we can ask or imagine" (Ephesians 3:20).

From the Fifth Ward to Spring Branch to Hotel Herrington, from schools to offices, from churches to a neighborhood near you, God's people are slowly and intentionally changing the narrative in and about the church. Jesus really is seeking the holistic shalom-peace of our cities!

This new story is possible here and now! Wanna join?

I'd like to leave you in the same place my book began—in worship. I have experienced God in my life and world and repeatedly find myself drawn to praise. I wrote this credo soon after I began writing this book, and I continue to find life in these words. Perhaps more than anything, I hope and pray my stories and testimony have encouraged you to believe!

I believe if God raised Jesus from the dead, then anything is possible.

Love is possible. Hope is possible. Joy is possible. Taking risks, overcoming fears, dealing with negative emotions and anxiety, moving beyond habitual disobedience—all are now possible.

The welcome and integration of strangers, extravagant generosity and simple living, serving the marginalized, working for the common good: these, too, are possible.

I believe if God brought Jesus back to life, then even I can change!

I believe if God is making the heavens new and the earth new, then all things are being renewed: individuals and churches, couples and families, institutions and corporations, cities and nations, the molecule and the cosmos.

I believe our world needs God's kingdom now more than ever. My friends, family, neighbors, and coworkers need God now. *I* need God's kingdom now, and I commit my life and energies to making it a reality.

And one day, when our prayers for the kingdom to come on earth are answered, justice, peace, and celebration will be the state of the union and the state of every human heart.

I believe God is making all things new! We are being transformed by God to transform the world.

Dear God, please start with me. Amen.

EPILOGUE

Ship of Theseus

WHILE WRITING *The Gospel Next Door*, I was reminded of the ancient riddle of the ship of Theseus. For centuries, philosophers have wondered whether a ship, if restored by replacing planks and mast, sails and rudders, until finally every single piece of the ship has been replaced, is still the same ship.

I wonder if that's true for me, because the book you're holding is not the book I set out to write. Correction: it's not the book that I *did* write—the first time. What was planted as a seed in 2013 has grown into something else entirely. The journey has seen every chapter transformed, every paragraph and sentence and word worked and reworked and worked again. The further I got into the journey, the more it changed, with the help of committed partners, the stories you've read here, and first-class editing from Valerie Weaver-Zercher (thank you!). But this was the book I needed to write, the book my Christian calling led me to write.

I've come to realize that mission—and life itself—is like that ship. We start off with an idea or inspiration and set out to do something good. Along the way we meet people who teach us what we didn't know we didn't know, and our lives are changed because of it. We surge ahead to overcome obstacles, then find ourselves thrown back against the rocks, needing to rebuild for the sake of survival. We try, we err, we grow, we err some more, we try some more, we fall more in love than we ever imagined. And at some point in our mission, we look back at the path we've taken and we have to ask: Am I the same person as when I started? Are we the same people who set off together so long ago? Is this the same book I pitched to my publisher?

I've seen people who have RSVP'd to Jesus' invitation and set off in a surprising direction, and though they may look back from time to time, they know they can never go back. Too much has happened on the journey, too much has changed—they've gone far enough that they'll never be the same. I've introduced you to some of these folks—Erica Reggatt, Julie Waters, Dominick Green, Hannah Bonner, Betty and Jim Herrington, and Kathryn and Dave Bauchelle, to name a few.

I think I'm on that kind of journey too. Though there are more planks in my life that need replacing than what have been replaced, and some are ready for a *re*-replacement, I'm learning to go where life takes me, to give up what I cannot keep, and to try and err and try again.

My church is also like that ship, as perhaps yours is too. The same can be said of my city, because of the influence of Christianity in our history.

The point isn't to get mission right the first time, to answer every question before you even begin, or even to know where you're going. The point is to go, preferably together, wherever your faith takes you. Please do go. Please do RSVP to Jesus' invitation. You've got so much that our world needs. Your neighbors want what you have and only Jesus can give. Your neighborhood and city and planet are hungry for a new spirituality and world. You've got an opportunity to change the story in and about the church and live the truth that Jesus is seeking the peace of our cities.

Nobody needs you to be perfect, so you can stop worrying about that. God's already got that covered. It's not your perfection they need; it's your presence. So go, follow Jesus. Follow Jesus not as keepers of a private God but as followers of a public way. Follow Jesus as a mother, neighbor, teacher, restaurant entrepreneur, or inmate in a Texas prison. Follow Jesus to the ends of the earth and into the halls of power. Go, follow Jesus wherever he leads you, especially if it's next door.

If you do, there's one thing I believe will be true for you— you'll never be the same.

Writing this book has been the most communal thing I've ever done. That wasn't by mistake, and it's not unique to people on mission. Early on I decided that my congregation, Houston Mennonite: The Church of the Sermon on the Mount, needed to have a huge influence on this project. That was, for me, the only way to imagine what it means to be an Anabaptist pastor and public theologian. I can't thank them all enough. Special thanks to Kathryn Hatfield Bauchelle and her graceful editing!

Houston has a starring role in this book because its people and churches inspire me with their stories of faithfulness. I think especially of the community of Faithwalkers and the joy in which they seek transformation. Jim Herrington has been without a doubt my biggest cheerleader and fan, and his brilliance and compassion are changing the way we make disciples. Thank you, Jim, for showing me grace and holding me to the truth.

The board and participants at Healing the Brokenness changed the way I saw the city, and none more than Joel Goza, whose pursuit of me as a close friend changed the way I saw myself and the quality of this project.

But what brought me back to pen and laptop was my family. I can't help but dream of a world where my kids live in shalom and of a time where they seek it passionately for others. Malakai, Clara, and Ruby: keep pretending and keep dreaming. The church needs people just like you.

My wife, Hannah, has been my rock, giving me permission and space and endless love. She has also rooted me in reality, reminding me that the real world of diapers, daughter dance parties, and date nights are the stuff of life—and a true gift from God.